CORPORATE SUPERPOWER:

Cultivating a Winning Culture for Your Business

Oleg Konovalov

CORPORATE SUPERPOWER published by:

WILDBLUE PRESS

P.O. Box 102440

Denver, Colorado 80250

WILDBLUE PRESS is registered at the U.S. Patent and Trademark Offices.

ISBN 978-1-947290-47-1 Trade Paperback

ISBN 978-1-947290-46-4 eBook

PRAISES

"The great Peter Drucker said, "Culture eats strategy for breakfast" and Oleg Konovalov shows why this is so true! Corporate Superpower can help your organization create the culture needed to move to the next level of success. Great coaching on culture from a great thinker!"

Marshall Goldsmith, Thinkers 50, #1 Leadership Thinker, #1 Executive Coach in the World

"In more than 20 years of working with companies around the world, I understand that culture is one of the most important, if not THE most important, determining factor in an organization's success. That is why I think it is essential that you read Corporate Superpower. This is book is among the most comprehensive, insightful and educational books I have ever read on how to build a

world-class culture. I consider this a must read on this extremely critical topic."

John Spence, Top 100 Business Thought Leader & Small Business Influencer in the USA

"Oleg Konovalov is a deep thinker. He explores the role and function of modern corporate culture, sharing plenty of practical, philosophical, and thought-provoking ideas that can take your business to the next level."

Shep Hyken, Customer Service Expert, NYT bestselling author of The Amazement Revolution

"Today many large and mega corporations spend a great deal of money and time trying to increase the originality of their employees, hoping thereby to get a competitive edge in the marketplace. The Book "Corporate Superpower" by Oleg Konovalov is a powerful tool and a critical ingredient to rethink modern corporate culture. No matter the industry or expertise, the visionary nature of "Corporate Superpower" will engage your team and strengthen your corporate environment.

"Corporate Superpower" exhibits an extraordinary transformative leadership

model that empowers CEO, managers, and employees, and helps understand the full spectrum of prioritizing the mental and emotional well-being of employees to increase profit, improve lives, transform culture, and sustain corporate growth. A modern business and society need such creative thinking and extraordinary approaches that allow making a leap forward and reaching new heights in development.

I have read "Corporate Superpower" twice and I am already experiencing the transforming powers of what leadership is all about, and how these principles can be integrated into the non-profit, businesses, small or large corporations, and government's best practice."

Hon. H.E. Sir. Dr. Raphael Louis, Founder, President/CEO FAAVM – AFPMV, Leader of the National Coalition Party of Canada

"A deeply compelling journey into the soul of successful organizations, from the Dark Kingdoms of dysfunctional company culture to the visionary heights of corporate superpowers. Rich with real life experiences, this book is an invaluable companion and guide for leaders, their organizations and

teams in times of increasing complexity and change."

David Clive Price, PhD, Expert on Global Leadership and Author of Bamboo Strong

"Indeed a very powerful book. The discussion of the essence of corporate culture, spiritual dimensions, and shared values is very illustrative and practical."

Sir Dr. Linjie Chou Zanadu, Secretary at the World Cultural Diversity Organization

"Corporate Superpower shares the secret that all world-class organizations have in common, they have amazing cultures. Your customers will never be any happier than your employees are. Oleg Konovalov tells you how to create an incredible corporate culture in this book."

John R. DiJulius III, Author of The Customer Service Revolution

"A graphically narrated book that connects the dots of the theory behind the practices that take place in the corporate world. A pragmatic and holistic review of all those elements that affect the employee experience. This book gives the impression to the

reader that is being mentored by a wise person that has the diverse experience and super power to navigate the reader through the contemporary workplace cultures. A valuable, practical guide for the uncharted geographies of the current and future work environment."

Anna Mamalaki, Global HR, Employee Experience Expert

"Dr. Oleg Konovalov offers a new word in culture management and unlocking potentials for the XXI century businesses. In his outstanding book, Oleg sets new standards of understanding corporate culture as the main source of inner energy and critical metaphysical resources which define sustainable development and long-term success. The offered discussion exceeds patterned thinking, yet practical and appealing. One of the best books on corporate culture."

H.E. Ms. Sania A. Ansari, Chair Person, Ansari Group Ltd.

Table of Contents

CORPORATE
SUPERPOWER:

ACKNOWLEDGEMENTS

This book would never have been completed without the encouragement and support of my loving and beautiful wife, Zagidat. She put up with me during the many late nights I spent researching and writing, and kept me going whenever things got difficult.

Insightful comments, critical notes, and overall support provided by Dr. Carmel de Nahlik have been invaluable and deserve special praise.

I am grateful to my inspiring teacher Professor Laszlo Polos for his invaluable lessons and the encouragement to look beyond traditional boundaries.

Special thanks to Eric Postma for his support, valuable editorial suggestions, and practical comments.

My appreciation to Sheri McInnis, as a bestselling author, for the support and experience she shared with me.

I would also like to thank all those who responded to my questions and enthusiastically shared their experiences, supported this project, and motivated me to continue this tough journey. They helped round out the concept that forms the heart of this book. Had they not graciously given their time and thought to their responses, this would have been a very different book.

To my son, Savva

INTRODUCTION

FACETS OF ORGANIZATIONAL CULTURE

Early morning, the alarm clock rings to a new day. The coffee is brewed, ready to inject energy into our bodies and minds. Are we feeling confident and motivated to face new challenges in the office or struggling to get out of the door, dreading the day ahead?

It depends primarily upon a mysterious and invisible component of every organization, present but different in each one – culture. Culture reveals the true nature of an organization, whether it is a positive one which encourages people to perform at their best, or a negative one, destructive towards their efforts and desires.

A Human's Presence in the Universe

The psychological qualities of love, trust, spirit, and courage are what make humans different from other living creatures. Residing in the mind and soul, these defining human attributes allow us to dream, create, progress, and survive in almost any environment. We not only observe and react to our environment but also interact with and manipulate it. We consciously change our environment to help us face life's challenges. We inherit some attributes, while developing others as we mature through various tests and trials. From these trials arise great philosophers, creators, and explorers.

When forming groups and businesses, people merge their psychological qualities into a cohesive identity, a culture. A positive culture holds people together, providing a common framework within which we interact with each other and the world around us. The first attempt to explain the meaning of culture was in the 1st century B.C. by the Ancient Roman philosopher and orator, Cicero, who used an agricultural metaphor *cultura animi* to explain the highest possible ideal for human development. In Cicero's view, culture is not bounded by the nation's frontiers, but spans much further.

In the days of the Roman Empire's glory, Julius Caesar spoke highly of Cicero's achievements, saying, "It is more important to have greatly extended the frontiers of the Roman spirit (*ingenium*) than the frontiers of the Roman Empire." Thus, culture is formed by groups or nations, and has a direct influence not only on those who form and live within its geographical boundaries, but also on all those who interact with that culture.

The meaning of culture did not change much through the centuries; the very word meant "place tilled" in Middle English, and the same word goes back to Latin *colere*, "to inhabit, care for, till, worship." Culture is the result of people's psychological interests, their understanding of human nature and of the world around them. In turn, culture influences people's behavior and attitudes and guides them in the satisfaction of their psychological needs. People often adopt habits from other cultures as well. This can be seen in the use of foreign languages, habits, clothes, food, and practices.

Culture influences people's actions and vision, minds and hearts, whether as a small group or an entire nation. In fact, one could say that an organization's culture is its soul, and whoever controls the culture controls the soul. Thus, controlling the culture has been a primary goal of leaders of all types throughout history.

In 1914, more than a century ago, the poet Osip Mandelshtam (Mandelshtam1973, 67) wrote in his untitled poem:

Let the names of flowery cities

Caress the ear with fleeting glory.

It is not Rome the city that's immortal,

But man's presence in the universe.

Kings try to get man in their power,

Priests find excuses for their wars,

And yet without him hearths and altars,

Like wretched rubble, are beneath contempt.

Defining Organizational Culture

Organizations, being live social organisms developed by humans, incorporate the psychological qualities of their members, forming them into the specific and unique psychological personality of the organization. This is known as organizational culture. Culture is unique for every organization and reflects the values, beliefs, and ethical principles of the organization's members and founders. Despite numerous attempts, no one has yet devised a single cohesive definition of organizational culture, as individual authors view this phenomenon from different perspectives. However, while each organization's culture is unique, there are many similarities.

From the *Organisational Anatomy* (Konovalov 2016, 71) standpoint, culture is viewed as a catalyst for performance, and can either strengthen the organization or weaken it. As it has a direct and crucial impact on the utilization of organizational resources and development of capabilities, culture gives energy and strength to an organization, allowing it to move forward successfully through the market's many challenges. Strong and productive culture stimulates the enhancement of productivity by homogenizing the best psychological qualities of employees, the sense of corporate unity and belonging, internal cooperation, and employees' loyalty, thus forming the organizational soul. Organizational culture is the most crucial ingredient of success, giving life to all of its many processes.

How does culture differ between organizations? People differ in their emotional and psychological richness; nations differ in their cultural diversity representing high and low-context cultures; and organizations also differ in terms of the diversity of professional context. For instance, think about medical consultants, seamen, priests, pilots, or stock exchange traders. We can envision the complex nature of their duties and understand they cannot be performed using a simple protocol or operation manual. The culture of organizations specializing in these spheres of activity can be viewed as high-context. Each word, the manner of interaction and professional language, reflects specific responsibilities, urgency of actions, uncertainty, and the overall complexity of business.

A human's character changes with maturity, particularly after the individual has gone through tough challenges and subsequent reflection on them. Adults leave teenage manners and habits behind, and then their values, norms, and principles reflect maturity. The same happens with organizations.

Culture matures with the organization, becoming prominent and clearly articulated.

Within and Beyond the Organization's Boundaries

We cannot see someone's soul nor feel a spirit, whether by observing a body or through an X-ray. We sense it while interacting with people. Likewise, the same happens within organizations. We cannot see it, but we can feel the spirit of the organization. A positive organizational culture motivates employees to achieve excellence, while enriching productive partnerships and customer relations, thus making the organization excel beyond its rivals. As culture and its influence span beyond the organizational boundaries, not only do the organization's members feel it, but all of the organization's stakeholders are able to sense it and are affected by it.

Sustainable development depends on an organization's ability to attract and retain the best people. However, unless the spirit or culture motivates people to stay and perform to the best of their abilities, an organization's development will be stunted. People are the main ingredient of all processes, and without good people and their qualities and effort, even the best thought-through processes will not be effective.

Different organizations have very contrasting cultures just as humans have very different personalities. As such, an organization's strength, performance, limits, and potential for development will all vary. One develops capacities for fighting and prosperity, where another is equipped only to follow a flow rather than to lead, picking up bad habits along the way. We've all more than likely heard about situations where someone big and physically strong has been outfought by someone of smaller size and weight. It all comes down to a strong character and the motivation to win. The same happens with organizations. A strong culture can help a small organization triumph where larger groups falter. For instance, Starbucks has grown from being a small company with a handful of coffee shops to dominate with thousands of franchises across the globe by using a strategy built on a strong team culture.

Today's competitive climate requires superiority in relationship skills in order to secure a smooth and efficient supply of critical resources. Companies seek out partners that are compatible in order to form a reliable and mutually productive relationship. We gain from productive relations dealing with partners within a positive culture. By contrast, dealing with an organization that has a negative culture is like hitting the proverbial brick wall. Strong, positive organizational culture facilitates well-developed relationship skills and integrity, whereas negative culture in partnerships not only affects mutual understanding, but also is problematic in terms of mutual support, leading to any number of difficulties.

As an organization's focal resource and the most important external stakeholders, customers are quite adept at being able to sense an organization's culture. As a result, their dealings with an organization directly affect their loyalty. Customers are direct consumers of an organization's culture, being affected by everything an organization does to retain them. It is widely understood that all organizations want customers to be focused on their own products and not on those of the competitor, increasing our market share and securing organic growth.

Counterproductive Culture or "Dark Kingdom"

Do "Dark Kingdoms," i.e. organizations with negative cultures, exist in the organizational world? Realistically, of course they do, but people tend to avoid talking about them. Most management literature tends to discuss culture in a positive or inspirational light, neglecting the fact that few organizations have "a totally bright personality." There is no empirical data on the percentage of organizations with a negative culture, but I'm sure we have all had experiences with companies that we now prefer to avoid. Undoubtedly, the number of such firms may be greater than we can imagine. As consumers, most of us have encountered incidents of lousy repair work, unreturned phone calls, and the like. Perhaps, if we work for such an organization, we could relate to a statement such as: "Successfully survived for a year, working for company X in the capacity of a manager, and it was like being behind the enemy frontline."

When an organization's culture is negative or demotivating in nature, it will not stimulate the generation of the driving energy that pushes the organization to continually grow and improve. Rather, it works as a destructive power which serves to limit organizational productivity and makes resource utilization processes excessively costly. Creativity, enthusiasm, cooperation, and mutual support are replaced by excessive control and inefficient internal coordination.

Corporate Ideology

The number of employees in large organizations can easily hit the population of some countries, such as, for instance, Walmart with 2.1 million employees, and thus these organizations can be considered as small states. Spanning countries and continents, such giants have a diverse culture consisting of a number of sub-cultures, some of which can come into conflict, making multi-national corporations seem schizophrenic or bi-polar at times. They demand a cultural core which would, theoretically, allow them to maintain solidarity for future decades, gain a sustainable strategic advantage, and consolidate strength and power, all of which feed back into the culture.

Supporting the longest-term strategies, corporate ideology must be goal-focused for the foreseeable future, and at the same time leave room for innovation. Ideology, the corporate doctrine which reflects and respects the cultural standards and desires of organizational members, aids in maintaining the organization's cultural and human standards at the highest level. It creates a long-lasting and supportive internal environment, helping grant purpose to and fulfillment of the personal aims of its citizens.

A Leader's Role

How is organizational culture formed and who forms it? Organizational culture is not inherited from previous generations like culture is in a society, but formed by the organization's founders and leaders who are the first generation of the micro-society. Culture is the result of conscious choices and efforts, rather than a slow development. They form the initial boundaries and rules responsible for shaping culture and nurturing it through the stages of the organization's maturity. Building a sustainable business and winning people's hearts will always remain key tasks for all leaders. The leaders' job is to make dreams come true and culture is the most versatile and powerful tool in their hands.

Corporate culture and leadership guru, John Mattone emphasizes, "The two key macro levels that make or break transformation efforts are culture and leadership" (Mattone 2016, 24) which reflects the critical role that leaders play as macro-forces in this tandem. However, culture is a double-edged sword and if it is not managed with great care and professionalism, leaders can easily become the destroyers rather the champions of an organization.

A leader can be a perfect strategist who is capable of moving horizons, but if this leader cannot feel and care for the corporate culture, success will remain illusory. Just as with a human soul, organizational culture demands exercise, regular maintenance, and careful development.

When feeling anxiety and psychological discomfort, we tend to rush to cure the problem by speaking with a psychologist, chatting with a friend, confessing to a priest, or simply reading a self-help book aimed at healing the soul's worries to make it stronger. An organization cannot go to a psychologist. In effect, a manager's role is to be the organization's psychologist, if you will, as it is the leader who diagnoses its ills and works to heal its psychological problems. Culture, or the psychological state of the organization, defines the productiveness of its internal environment. The last thing we want to see is for it to be fragmented.

Unfortunately, the duty of cultural caretaking frequently appears at the very bottom of a list of priorities, or is oftentimes completely neglected. Managers tend to think that employees' respect and loyalty can be taken for granted, which leads to the development of a negative or counterproductive culture. For instance, looking at the structure of some organizations we can see strongholds which actually separate managers from their own people, hence discouraging cultural unity inside the organization. It is the duty of the manager to enrich and stimulate the development of the organizational soul by cultivating and nurturing real values and appropriate attributes which are valued and respected by all employees. If leaders concentrate on the application of fake, inappropriate attributes, such characteristics will lead to the organization's self-destruction.

A number of questions arise. What are the factors and qualities that demand the most attention and care? What values are the most relevant in the specific context of an organization? What attributes are primary and which are secondary? How can we treat culture to make it advantageous?

A Superpower

Aristotle stated (Aristotle 2012), "We are what we repeatedly do. Excellence, then, is not an act but a habit." Differences in quality of resources, environmental and market changes, and technological progress lead to a rethinking of an organization's processes. However, this consistency of organizational development and level of performance cannot be achieved without positive organizational culture, which is a superpower in itself. Only with such a culture can the desired excellence be achieved on a consistent basis.

Similar to the human soul, organizational culture is non-tangible. We cannot touch it, but we feel its presence; we either sympathize with or reject it. Most organizational processes are measurable and rational, whereas culture has more of a metaphysical nature and often seems irrational. Thus, it is difficult to measure and cannot be changed by a snap of the fingers, yet it defines and focuses all the energy and activity in an organization.

Symbols and values are actual drivers and stimulators that define the direction of organizational development. Attributes are responsible for supporting values and making them visible to members of a given organization. If values and attributes are not formulated correctly, then the organization is at risk of not achieving a desired level of performance. The most difficult task for leaders in this context is to formulate values and attributes which will be effective and relevant on a long-term strategic horizon.

Organizational culture is often ignored at the cost of losing control over the organization, which then will become ineffective and unable to perform, eventually leading to organizational death. Certainly, we do not want culture to become a processes inhibitor which works against organizational goals. Therefore, periodical examinations of organizational culture must be conducted, which can only be done based on a clear understanding of its nature. Just as a human heals and strengthens different facets of their soul in terms of personal development, all organizations need to review and revise the state of their culture on a regular basis.

In the words of Marshall Goldsmith (Goldsmith 2015, 38), "No one can make us change unless we truly want to change." Dear reader, are you prepared to mistreat or ignore this invisible ingredient of your business success? This book will discuss factors defining and shaping organizational culture, symptoms of counterproductive culture, cultural values and attributes, specific cultural qualities of organizations, corporate ideology, the role of leaders in defining and maintaining culture in their organizations, and culture-related risks and problems. It is for those who value people and aim to enhance the superpower of organizational culture, boosting performance as a result.

CHAPTER ONE

LIVE, IMMATERIAL, AND FUNCTIONAL

Since the time of Cicero, people have tended to take the phenomenon of culture for granted, often assuming that it is synonymous with organizational culture. However, a more specialized understanding of organizational culture began to coalesce some decades ago. In fact, it was first described as a group climate by Lewin, Lippitt, and White in 1939. Subsequently, in the mid-seventies, organizational norms, roles, and values were viewed in terms of the social psychology of organizations, although, at that stage, it was not explicitly stated as organizational climate or culture. Since then, a large number of definitions have appeared, serving to confirm the complex nature of this incorporeal being. However, we are still exploring this elephant in a dark room.

Culture does not exist in an isolated and purified environment without the presence of other people. Culture is a complex phenomenon, deeply interpenetrating all of our daily activities, which exists only in collectives of people, i.e. in states, nations, and organizations. Culture is a system itself. The word "system" derives from the ancient Greek word *systema* which comes from two words – *syn*, which means "together", and *histemi*, which means "to set." System is actually an idea which defines how process or ideology is to be set for the best possible performance or outcome. Cultural or ideological systems can be seen as a collection of roles which reflect human values and thus have a direct impact on organizational results. As a system, culture needs to be viewed using a systematic approach and not a mono-dimensional view.

Three Dimensions of Culture

Culture is multidimensional. One dimension is pragmatic and rational, regulating rules, norms, and codes of working in organizations. A second dimension is more irrational and incorporates the behavioral and psychological approach of the group's members to their duties and to the organization itself. A third dimension reflects the transcendent side of culture, which can be viewed as the organizational cathedral, the reference point for the entire organization's activity.

Regarding the strictly rational aspect, Aristotle wisely defined a state, as an interaction for reaching mutual goals. Not short-term tasks, but goals of successful survival, prosperity, mutual support, defense, and satisfaction of its own needs. Applying

Aristotle's definition to an organizational viewpoint, we can say that it is similar to the purpose of the state, just on a smaller scale – an organization is the interaction of its members ordered to reach defined goals that benefit the organization.

Organisational Anatomy (Konovalov 2016, 71) defines organizational culture as a catalyzer of performance. I will use this definition in the present discussion as being the most advanced and practically relevant to the aims of all organizations. Looking at the spiritual or transcendent side, we can consider company culture as the soul of the organizational body, which helps the brain (management) motivate the body for action, sense the environment, attract stakeholders' positive emotions and energy, stimulate and encourage development, and drive the organization through tough times.

This third dimension is the dynamic power and spiritual core of the organization. It is built on symbols which shape the company's psychological state and define the boundaries of its influence. We will discuss the role of symbols and values in more detail later as this is a tremendously critical and under-appreciated issue.

Each of these facets of organizational culture empowers and enlightens the other sides of the immaterial core of any company, and by doing so, gives life and vitality to a company. Culture also defines the boundaries of an organization. Within those boundaries, dependent upon the culture's nature, the talents of the employees are revealed and allowed to flourish.

Indispensable Catalyzer

Production or providing of services can be compared with a complicated chemical reaction of long-chain utilization of resources by perfectly synergized functions. A chemical reaction is a change of two components – substance and energy. Substance, in this sense, represents all tangible and intangible resources and capabilities within an organization. Organizational culture is that energy which comes from the joint efforts and enthusiastic fulfillment of duties of all employees, and, as a result, adds spark and life to all processes. If the culture is positive and stimulating, then we can expect the desired reaction which results in a superior product and secures growth.

At the same time, we do not want culture to be a counterproductive energy, i.e. an inhibitor, which slows down substance transformation, making resource utilization costly and restricting the organization's growth. In a more rigorous way, there is a fit between strategy and culture which has a direct impact on company performance.

In a positive cultural environment, we become more productive and positively attuned toward colleagues. We speak with enthusiasm to friends about what we do, how important it is, and how good it is to work for our company. If the organization's members are effectively collaborating, positively and naturally attuned toward achieving company goals, this positive energy will aid in creating excellent products even if the materials used are less than perfect. Using culture to generate this level of enthusiasm and commitment is important for any company, established or start-up. Strong culture allows enhanced exploitation of people's competencies, reaching higher behavioral consistency among employees, and overall preparedness for necessary change.

Immortal Soul

A strong soul defines a healthy psychological state and provides strength. If one is going through challenges at a stage when muscles are prepared to give up, the soul pushes forward and thus achieves success. Also, it is important to understand that a company and its culture cannot be separated just as a human being and a soul cannot function independently of each other.

A group of people, even when working toward the same goal, remains a crowd without this intangible, yet vital, element of culture. Culture serves as a force which forms productive and collaborative teams. Culture is born as soon as founders start actively interacting in the creation of a business plan and establishing a new venture, even before the organization is fully formed. They are imprinting the first characteristics of culture, its nature and shape. Unfortunately, the issue of culture is usually a neglected conversation by entrepreneurs and start-up enthusiasts, often at the cost of a slow and ineffective start-up. Entrepreneurs and investors need to look into the cultural properties of a new project as a matter of priority, for in so doing, they will define future growth prospects which can predict future performance.

Spiritual Core

The spiritual core defined by culture is responsible for a sense of belonging, loyalty, pride, and a number of other crucial factors of productive organizational citizenship. Residing in symbols and a proclaimed understanding of the need for effective interaction towards organizational goals, cultural identity in any organization is as unique as human fingerprints and cannot be replicated anywhere else.

When we talk about a person we admire, a common characteristic we note is that this person is able to pull him or herself together when facing difficulties. A person who exhibits such spiritual strength is able to deliver extraordinary performance and reveal inner creativity in the face of adversity.

The same applies in businesses where spiritual identity permeates all operations and processes, forming a solid dome above a company, allowing it to withstand any problem. However, if a company's spiritual identity is weak, it is like being under a leaky shelter, eventually driving its people away.

A Rationality of Immaterial Being

A tree with roots that grow deep can withstand strong winds. The stronger and deeper the roots, the stronger the tree is. We cannot see these roots, but we can see the tree. If the roots are weak then the tree will have more of a withered appearance with a lot of dead branches. Likewise, organizational culture becomes strong only if it's built on action and interaction, i.e. active and effective collaboration and mutual support, and not just talking about possible success.

Managers tend to neglect to form an understanding of organizational culture and the vital role it plays in making the organization successful. Most often, managers receive training about leadership styles, ways to motivate staff, and corporate loyalty. Rarely does this involve discussions of the foundational role culture plays in a company. As a result, businesses face constant loss of seemingly loyal customers, valuable employees, and enthusiastic investors. We are consciously digging a pothole for the companies by turning toward seemingly rational opportunistic transactions. However, pure rationality is not enough in the management of such sensitive issues as loyalty, staff motivation, and customer satisfaction. In terms of internal environment, culture bridges a gap between purely functional working relationships and interpersonal relationships which are a substratum for nurturing tacit knowledge, reciprocity, and willingness to understand others.

Rationally bound actions often result in quick gains but often become less successful in the long term. The metaphysical role of culture in this phenomenon is underestimated. Without culture, all these aspirations and seemingly feasible plans become unrealistic.

Organizational culture has a tremendous number of roles due to its trifold nature. Culture is everywhere and in everything, from how people support colleagues, care for customers, solve problems, respect company achievements, and even to how a cup of coffee is offered to a visitor. We can feel a company's culture right from our first interaction with it. Culture gives a human appearance to the living body of an organization, thus making it attractive in the eyes of employees and customers. Its uniqueness can be seen in the organization's determination, persistence in achieving goals, desire for development, and spirit of creativity and innovation.

As Japanese writer Ryunosuke Satoro concisely stated, "Individually, we are one drop. Together, we are an ocean." By strengthening bonds between co-workers, culture makes them an ocean with a tremendously irresistible power to achieve phenomenal goals. If employees feel respected and appreciated, they no longer feel like separated drops but important parts of a greater whole, and as a result, they feel obliged to be productive, loyal, and engaged in company life. These critical attributes are seeded and nurtured by culture. Also, culture provides an adaptation mechanism which shapes and adjusts the mindsets of new recruits and revitalizes company veterans in line with organizational goals, thus securing stable long-term development.

Organizational processes and relations cannot be harmonic without a prominent positive culture. People-centered culture encourages an environment of collaboration, stimulating development of seamless and harmonic organizational processes. It is the key to balancing collective and individualistic behaviors and uniting them for one purpose.

Trust is the glue and stimulator of all relations, and no authentic business transaction can be executed without it. Trust is a macro-phenomenon which lubricates all internal and external processes. It strengthens relationships inside and outside the organization, helping to develop mutual support. A strong culture stimulates trust across the entire organization, building it from within and from without. By contrast, a weak culture is characterized by a breakdown of trust that will see the organization dissolve into isolated cliques with little to no communication between them.

Culture, and its transformations over a company's history, reflects the experiences of surviving in a challenging organizational environment. It reflects how organizational members have gone through extreme moments, withstood external forces, collaborated, and learned from each other. Thus, culture derives from a combination of the reflection of bad experiences, best practices, and advantages of mutual support.

For instance, a co-founder of a British transport company suggested that:

"We took care to nurture a supportive environment from day one that eventually allowed us to survive, learn from losses, value the role of each team member, learn how to work through socializing and become stronger as one body. Expensive trucks are nothing without effective people."

It is impossible to develop such human and social capitals without culture, which is critical for organizational existence. Human capital represents skills, talents, knowledge, experience, creativity, and know-how, which can flourish only in an environment of positive culture. By stimulating mutual support and development of productive internal and external organizational relations, culture is a great constructor of social capital which allows attracting resources embedded in external networks of relations. Culture makes an organization a social being and a responsible part of a society, which aids in attracting additional external support and the recognition of its contributions.

Functions of Culture

A modern American skeptic and writer, Phil Plait, in his talk *The Goal of Skepticism*, noted, "Give a man a truth and he will think for a day. Teach a man to reason and he will think for a lifetime." (Plait 2010) By understanding the reasons behind the very nature of organizational culture and its functions, we obtain food to fuel our thoughts and actions for a lifetime.

Let's imagine the product of a given business as a gold bar valued according to purity. It could be a product unit for producers, money or knowledge for knowledge-dependent organizations, the number of served customers for location-dependent organizations, saved lives for charities, or tax-paying citizens in a state. An equation to express the relationship between the gold and the activity which generates it would work by multiplying product units by hours worked, in which the product unit is something physical offered to customers. However, we also can add effort, motivation, or commitment into this equation as elements from another immeasurable and undefined dimension – the strength of organizational culture. The equation will then read: product unit x hours x cultural strength which will result in a gold bar of 24-karat value. However, should the culture be counterproductive, i.e. have negative value; the value of the final product will be significantly reduced.

It is common to think that a product only comes out of a workshop as the result of physical resources and energy. Such an outlook overlooks the psychological components of the organization. Understandably, it is easy to concentrate on what we can see, and touch; tangible items that we can fix. However, the real strength of any organization comes not from its physical resources but from more intangible, more qualitative elements.

We can define culture as organizational metaphysics. This is the physics of managing human emotions and senses. The difference between successful and unsuccessful business lies in understanding this.

The inner psychological state of the organization is reflected in the functions of culture. The functions are: the inner organization's language, praxis or active doing, apoptosis or controlled cells death, homeostasis or cultural system regulator, and entropy or energy regulator. We will discuss these critical functions in greater details further in this chapter.

Language

Culture differs based on context. Whether we walk into a university, church, fishmonger shop, or a Navy ship, there will be differences in culture, an often-overlooked reality. The clearest difference is that each organization has its own unique language. By recalling Terry Pratchett's *The Colour of Magic* (2008), we may say that the organizational universe is full of different discs with their own cultures and thus their own standards and languages. From this viewpoint, language reflects a nature, structure, and description of roles in a cultural domain.

Language defines the art of transmitting and reading signals between people. Language defines communication as a vehicle of transmitting messages and stories between people without losing the quality of human emotions and perspectives. It defines the use of acceptable and forbidden metaphors. Language describes values and allows them to be communicated to all corners of the cultural territory.

Consider legendary hero Jason and his Argonauts in their chase for the Golden Fleece. All their challenges and obstacles were successfully overcome for two main reasons – creative actions and extraordinary communication. This allowed great understanding among the Argonauts, and negotiations with unusual and not always friendly people and creatures. We can see how communication makes language alive and functional like wind in the sails.

Talking about past, present, and forthcoming events, people engage their minds and hearts to shape their future. Socialization, which is much needed for maintaining effective relationships and mutual support, is defined by the quality of communication. Picking up facts and impressions from an organization's memory and people's experiences and communications develops shared affection. Communication is necessary to leverage human desires and feelings and to marshal numerous opinions to work for the organization's purposes. Critical factors such as involvement, engagement, and integration can't be developed without effective communication.

Strong culture is defined by a clear language of communication. Thus, professionalism is reflected in simple language. By contrast, negative culture reflects event- or trend-driven or spontaneous meanings and words which tend to change from occasion to occasion. To be a positive force in the organization, language must be very specific, commonly accepted, and constant, changing only as necessary.

Communication is responsible for interaction with the external world, helping the organization to learn about customers' tastes, needs, and desires, and to talk with them about the products and services available. High performing organizations show an advanced level of communication. Effective and purposeful communication is a sign of intelligence that can't be replicated by poorly formed competitors. Having a dynamic nature, communication allows development by talking through processes bolt by bolt, operation by operation, and stage by stage, securing intelligent performance and goal achievement.

Active Doing, or Praxis

Managing emotions and responsibility encourages the engagement of all members in organizational development, applying new processes and practicing skills and competencies on a perpetual basis. In other words, we are talking about a process of organizational praxis, or with reference to Aristotle, active doing through the employment of skills which are fully enacted and realized.

When talking about positive and negative organizational cultures, we need to consider that praxis, or active doing, can differ in its nature, and not always lead to positive results. Only if a positive culture exists in a company can we talk about good *praxis*, or *eupraxia*. In eupraxia, people collaborate together, committing to company goals and being fully engaged in the organization's life. Doing so will secure dynamic development and excellent results for years to come.

If a counterproductive culture has conquered an organization, those without a clear understanding of culture will generally regard it as nothing more than bad luck, or dyspraxia. Such an organization has left behind any attempt to enact change. Any dynamism there once was has long since gone. Its members may look busy, but their hearts and minds are not engaged and the whole organization will continue to drift further and further from its original vision and principles. No organization can continue on this trajectory long before it dies.

Maintaining a positive culture is of paramount importance for an organization's existence and sustainable development. Doing so requires active choices and continued effort on the part of the organization's owners, investors, and managers. These choices include actively putting the organization's values into practice. To avoid this choice is to choose to merely be a victim of happenstance, a prisoner of fortune, or misfortune. Such inaction will be sure to lead to a swift death.

Leaders love talking about synergy, often pointing to results in which one plus one seems to equal three. This cannot be possible with only physical resources. An unseen element is necessary. Praxis, or active doing, is that invisible element responsible for the development of this desired extra value.

Revitalization, or Apoptosis

Thinking about an organization as a living body drives us to consider a peculiar process – *apoptosis*, the phenomenon of programmed cell death. This process is normal and necessary, allowing for new cells to grow and develop. More than fifty billion cells die in a human body every day. It is a process we do not even notice.

The same process happens in organizations. People come and go; the quality of resources is never exactly the same; processes are never perfect; and market changes play their own serious role in shaping the organization. We cannot stop this phenomenon and should not try to. Just as it is for us, apoptosis is good for an organization. In a positive culture, apoptosis allows for the deleting of damaged, infected, or mutated cells and ensures the effective functioning of the immune system. We all know people who are in excellent physical and mental shape even at a very advanced age because of their strong personalities. Organizations are the same. It is great to work for, or partner with, an organization with a positive culture that remains strong and focused from its inception into old age.

Negative apoptosis, being a property of a strong culture, allows the organization to remain in peak condition. Positive or defective apoptosis is characterized by the uncontrolled proliferation of cells, causing horrible diseases such as atrophy and cancer. Biologists distinguish two pathways in which positive apoptosis can flow – intrinsic and extrinsic. In organizational terms, a number of diseases are accredited to it. We see these diseases taking root in a counterproductive culture.

As soon as people in any given department face a stressful situation, this will cause a reaction down the intrinsic pathway and this organizational cell will inevitably kill itself. With the negative signal spreading around the organization, the extrinsic pathway takes charge and all organizational cells are reprogrammed for death. For instance, employing an increasing number of unprofessional and unethical employees is a precursor to positive apoptosis.

Negative culture management of this kind creates a sense of meaninglessness which leads to a positive apoptosis, triggering the growth of organizational 'parasites' who are like cancer cells, causing the business to suffer further. Unprofessional and unethical people, as aggressive aliens, view a company's culture and use it only for quick personal gain. Such people tend to grow in numbers, slowly killing the company from the inside. An outsider can often detect the resultant atmosphere and will look elsewhere for places to take their business.

Self-Detection, or Homeostasis

As soon as we talk about culture as a system which is responsible for the inner organizational environment, we must consider that every system has compulsory properties. A strong system is a composition of well-regulated and productive elements. A faulty or weak system reflects that its inner elements are unbalanced and damaged.

In biological terms, the inner harmony of different roles and functions and other variable elements is regulated by a property known as *homeostasis*. Homeostasis is a physiological mechanism responsible for detecting deviations in elements not functioning in accordance with assumed standards, deleting damaged cells, and the correction of errors or malfunctioning elements.

A positive culture plays a role similar to homeostasis in an organizational context, regulating inner relations, balancing and stimulating knowledge and information sharing, enhancing competences, and warning against people's misbehavior. For instance, if culture stimulates knowledge sharing then results will be seen in advanced organizational competences. In a counterproductive culture, homeostasis will not function properly, thus organizational competencies will not be developed due to a damaged knowledge and information flow.

Culture is a psychological regulator of the complex inner organizational world. It keeps an organization's communication channels open and stimulating. If damaged due to a negative culture, communications loops become low or broken altogether. Without good communication, no clear understanding or tacit knowledge can be developed amongst employees.

I enjoyed watching the effects of homeostasis on a team in a Starbucks' coffee shop in Birmingham, England, which I visited on a daily basis for a couple of years. My experience was the same every time. People were supportive of each other, flexible in their duties, and treated their jobs with respect, taking responsibility for everything that happened there. I heard a barista talking to a new member of staff about the preferences of the regular customers, and saw the manager professionally solving a conflict with a non-sober customer. The environment in this shop was as warm and enjoyable as the cup of fresh coffee I got there every day; the strong culture of the team demonstrating homeostasis at its best. Needless to say, this location makes plenty of money for its owners along with good memories for customers.

Damaged homeostasis reflects such organizational diseases as cross syndrome, incoordination syndrome, tie atrophy, and stiffness which are discussed in *Organisational Anatomy* (Konovalov 2016, 150). Organizational metabolism is responsible for the growth of the organization and its responsiveness to the environment and itself is directly dependent on the peculiar role of culture of homeostasis.

Self-Regulating, or Entropy

An effective organization is a fist of concentrated energy contributed by every employee and directed towards the achievement of particular goals, guaranteeing high performance. These individual inputs vary in their quality and value. It is great when all streams of energy are pure and synchronized. However, problems arise when inputs turn negative and are contradictory in nature. Useful energy could be dissipated or simply wasted due to underperforming departments. In practical terms, it means low performance with well-known negative consequences.

Any organization has boundaries, resource limitations, a certain number of people involved, prescribed patterns of processes, and time horizons to produce value in terms of products or service.

Quality of resources, expertise, and variations in demand can lead to an enormous number of configurations influencing the result of an organization's activity for better or worse. In real terms, not all employees may act in accordance with assigned roles, and their expertise can be far from adequate to execute a business model successfully. A thoroughly planned business becomes nothing more than a funny computer game for them.

Consistent excellence in production and competitiveness demands teamwork, advanced knowledge, and competences in applying it. A professional and collaborative environment exists only in organizations with a positive culture. Such collaboration will result in the constant improvement of processes. In a negative culture, the organization's elements don't work well and the best they do is to try to fix already broken processes. An organization in this kind of shape will find it very difficult to move from a weak to a strong culture.

How can we understand these inconsistencies and disorders from an organizational culture standpoint? Here, the laws of thermodynamics offer insight, specifically concerning *entropy*. Entropy is a measure of the number of configurations that a system can have when in a state specified by certain microscopic variables. It often reveals a system's disorders.

Entropy is a function of an intelligent cultural system, one which should be self-regulating. It signals if any energy is wasted which is restricting the company from further development. How does it work? As an example, Special Forces troops demonstrate prominent entropy in their internal culture. They have zero tolerance for an underperforming team member regardless of rank, are famous for superior tactical knowledge, support the weakest and wounded in battle, and everyone performs together toward a common goal. They are masters of collaboration. Those who do not comply with the team's culture are immediately spotted, expelled, and actions are taken to restore the team's performance capacity.

Organizational preparedness for change, flexibility, and endurance are directly associated with entropy which allows a company to withstand challenges. Any organization or state in which culture accommodates entropy can be considered a winner. It can be sure that its own internal culture will generate the best possible solution when problems inevitably arise.

Counterproductive cultures simply lack entropy as a property. They tolerate misbehavior, inconsistencies in processes, and patchy collaboration, all of which destroy a company without mercy. Such a culture does not have an ingrained function of maintaining reliable and flexible systems capable of offering appropriate configurations of expertise, knowledge, and competences when needed.

Focus on People

Nineteenth-century German writer Johann Wolfgang von Goethe stated, "The way you see people is the way you treat them, and the way you treat them is what they become." Any organization is a complex living body consisting of members with different personal, intellectual, and psychological qualities. Therefore, each member plays a unique part in an organization's symphony. The issue is that in an orchestra, members can hear each other, enjoying performing and satisfying listeners. In most organizations, this aspect is not always prominent. Again, culture plays the role of a catalyzer responsible for recovering or restoring losses which occur during a transfer of cultural values and meaning from owners and leaders to organizational members.

To a great extent, culture should be considered as a helping hand for people who are adapting to a company environment. If positive and strong, then culture acts as a garden where people's natural qualities and desires are cultivated for their own benefit as well as that of the organization.

Culture is only productive if centered on stimulating people, growing each individual in the process, and helping them to reach the organization's goals; otherwise, it becomes abusive and destructive. In other words, people-centered culture leads to productivity, and the lack thereof, leads to a negative culture of disillusionment. We have all encountered cashiers or service providers who cannot answer our questions or are not willing to satisfy even minor requests, invoking purported company policy. This turns customers, stakeholders, and partners away. I would suggest that these service providers are not happy responding in this way, sounding unprofessional and feeling incapable of helping. Additionally, it fosters little chance for productive relationships and collaboration among employees. People enjoy performing and revealing their best qualities and skills in an environment which allows enhancement of their professional and life experiences with humanistic goals which go beyond mere profit.

As soon as the focus of culture is shifted from people, i.e. employees, customers, and partners, onto something else, such as processing systems or automated customer relationship management, then culture stops being a positive force. Turning attention away from people is like placing a sign on an organization's entrance door which shouts "We disrespect you!"

Positive culture is a reflection of an organization's respect for employees and external stakeholders. People will respect a company that respects them; no one will respect a company that does not respect them. As a result, people will not give their best effort as employees or patronize such a company as customers. In simple words, if employees feel respected and appreciated they become more productive, more loyal, more obliged to work effectively, and more engaged in company life.

Gain or Lose

Let's imagine that you have bought a very advanced gadget at a hefty price. Then you use it only as a fancy accessory, ignoring the practical use that you paid top dollar for. With time, many of the features become outdated and the device loses its appeal.

A similar scenario often happens in businesses where managers are not fully realizing the role of culture. As a result, the most powerful means of mass inspiration, encouragement, and company enrichment is not appropriately exploited. These managers seem to mistakenly assume that because culture does not have a price tag like a piece of software or company car, then it is not a valuable investment of time and resources, and will take care of itself, which is a drastically mistaken point of view.

Culture is intangible, but valuable and critical in terms of the company's existence and success. Yet, it can't be analyzed using first-order logic as it contains too many variables, and, therefore, is not simply something to manage. The complexity of culture makes people suspicious and skeptical, as they are not usually prepared to shift the dimensions and patterns of their thinking. However, complexity is merely a pack of simple items which are manageable if divided into digestible parts and elements.

This demands a view from other angles. The reason for discussing the functions of organizational culture as critical properties in such a manner is to offer a sophisticated view, allowing leaders to gain a superior understanding of the very nature of culture as its metaphysical nature often remains invisible to leaders and those still climbing the ladder. It is difficult to manage culture without an intimate understanding of its properties and functions.

If you desire to strengthen your business by adding strategic value, unique competitive advantage, and extra capacity, then taking care of organizational culture is a starting point on this journey to success.

CHAPTER TWO

DARK KINGDOMS OF COUNTERPRODUCTIVE CULTURE

Most of us have experienced periods darkened with dull mornings, few smiles, and constant stress while working for companies which do not exhibit the ideals we have been discussing. These are the Dark Kingdoms. At first, the excitement of a new role and bright plans make us eager to start the workday, but the enthusiasm quickly wanes when we discover the depressing reality.

A sketch of the Dark Kingdom is made in the dreary colors of a tense and unfriendly environment, competition over everything (except that which the leaders consider important), a feeling of eternal weariness, professional dissatisfaction, overwhelming formalities, and a certainty that all things will remain uncertain. Job fulfillment is just a fantasy. If this sounds like a past experience or describes your current job, don't worry. Keep smiling as it has a positive side – people in such jobs tend to spend more time with family and friends.

There is no statistical data on the numbers of good and bad people who live in the world. The same is true with organizations; no one can say with certainty how many companies have a bad corporate culture. Dark Kingdom companies have an organizational culture just like any other company, but it's negative. Negative or counterproductive culture does not reward people for high performance and commitment; rather, it is an inhibitor of positive organizational growth. Governance, transaction, and production costs grow constantly, leaving little chance for company survival. On a personal level, a bad personality is a problem for a few; on an organizational level, it is a problem for many.

Don't Talk Badly about the Almost Dead

The internet is full of articles discussing organizational culture from different perspectives, but only a few discuss the reality of a negative culture. In my research, I discovered that academic libraries offer almost 450,000 articles relevant to the study of organizational culture, and fewer than one hundred of them speak of negative culture. Maybe it is not noble to talk about something that is almost dead?

The first discussions about the negative role of organizational culture were initiated by Christina

Maslach in *Understanding Burnout* (Maslach 1982), referencing an influential model of burnout in the workplace consisting of three parts - emotional exhaustion, depersonalization, and diminished personal accomplishment. Emotional exhaustion results from daily stresses in a workplace culminating in a chronic state of depletion; depersonalization is a reflection of colleagues distancing themselves from each other and clients; and diminished personal accomplishment is a result of a negative self-evaluation provoked by a depressing working environment.

However, the tendency to give a low priority to discussions about negative culture prevails even now. People prefer to keep silent, seemingly afraid of destroying the remains of already fragile relationships and not wanting to risk being negatively labelled. Thus, employees don't talk about problems, and their leaders are not interested in talking about problems either. The risk of devaluation of the business is too great. One of the unwritten rules of business appears to be that the person who brings up a problem is the problem.

Discussing his experience of working in a Dark Kingdom, a department manager said:

"I hate what is going on in my company but I will keep quiet, not risking my job with only a few years left before retirement. I cannot talk with my boss about problems with culture as

it comes from him; I cannot talk with my staff for fear of being called insubordinate."

Forty or fifty years ago, when cancer was not easily treatable, it was considered a terminal sentence. Now, with more successful treatments available, people are more open to freely discussing it. I can only assume that if we were to learn and talk more about negative culture in business, then managers would be more successful in curing unhealthy companies.

Dark Kingdom, Dark Future

Negative culture is as dangerous as cancer for a company because it metastasizes slowly, ruining the whole body of a company and causing major lapses in organizational behavior. The company slowly rots from the inside out – ineffective internal relations, minimal commitment, low performance rates, and meaningless procedures begin to eat away at the morale and dedication of employees. From another angle, such organizational diseases as incoordination syndrome and cross syndrome, recognized by *Organisational Anatomy* (Konovalov 2016, 148-155), are rife. No insurance company will rush to issue an insurance certificate for a client with similar health conditions, and investors view emotionally risky businesses the same way. Underperforming companies are quickly removed from the market as they cannot satisfy the minimum level of performance, and they become an easy target for competitors. Investing in such a company is a risky bet.

Counterproductive culture is harmful for all internal and external stakeholders in different ways - dysfunctional culture, negative motivation, limited support, unwillingness to perform, lack of collaboration and team work, poor performance of "chosen" managers, misleading instructions and inadequate training, harmful impact on partners' reputations, and so on. For instance, discussing an experience working in a negative culture, one of my respondents from a large British fundraising company shared his story:

"This is probably my saddest experience working for a company which was supposed to be friendly to its own people and love those who donated. But it was quite often the complete opposite. We were knocking on doors and signing people up for regular donations using direct debit forms for a few big cancer charities. We received quick training and were sent out to the streets in teams of three to five with a team leader. I was assigned to a team led by M. who had worked there a long while and was considered one of the best in the branch.

The very first instruction we received from her was, "You must forget about ethics and other crap like this. Your job is to get money and sign-ups from people."

This was shocking. Then we noticed that she was lying to people at the doors, giving them false information about the charities for which we were collecting donations, and simply being rude to people. For instance, I witnessed M. saying to a woman whose child was crying, causing her to rush back into the house, "Your child isn't about to die, so you must talk with me."

We reported these cases, but it appeared that the managers were fully aware of such unethical behavior and the team leaders' attitude towards fundraisers and people, which was fairly standard. All was fine as long as the sign-up rate was achieved. Even more, managers were viewing it as a game, not thinking that the reputations of socially important charity-partners were under threat. More or less, well-known charities placed their hard-won reputation into the hands of gamblers whose own people were not encouraged to perform to their best. The performance rate dropped in fundraising campaigns, and the community was arrogant towards fundraisers. People quit the job daily and the working environment was horrible. I hated myself for working for this company and do not want to put it on my CV."

Who Pays the Price?

The price for a nerve-racking, anti-human environment is hefty for all – the company itself, employees, customers, and partners. The main problem is that a counterproductive culture is costly to the organization and separates people instead of uniting them.

Castle Wardens

Whatever resources are poured into a company with a counterproductive culture, it is still bound to underperform. The best strategic initiatives will crash against a wall of unethical behavior, irresponsibility, internal conflicts, unmotivated people, and fragmented processes. It may live for a long time, like the Dark Kingdom from a fairy tale, but it will be very costly for shareholders to keep it going.

John Sheridan published research in 1992 wherein he showed that "the cultural effects are estimated to have resulted in over six million dollars' difference in human resource costs between firms with different cultural values." (Sheridan 1992, 1038) Considering the difference in terms of pay rates, inflation, cost of businesses, etc. between 1992 and the present time, we may assume that this figure has increased dramatically.

People are resource carriers for any organization and they share these resources most willingly if appropriately motivated. No company can create economic capital without human knowledge, talents and personal qualities, and effective socioeconomic relations which form social capital. If not motivated and cared for, people keep their resources close to their chests, and therefore do not enrich the company to its fullest. They do not feel obliged to sacrifice something valuable to such an employer except very occasionally or for personal gain. However, the company remains at constant risk of losing value as people carry resources away with them simply by walking away from such organizations.

The line between legal and ethical is often thin, thereby allowing deviations when management interprets the company rules to employees. Unfortunately, in counterproductive cultures, the attention is often shifted towards the legal. This risks crossing another thin line between the counterproductive tendency of the organization's rules, which may seem legal decision-making, and real, ethical care of employees and customers.

In the case of Dark Kingdoms, cultural energy is not positive, but rather becomes an inhibitor which slows the chemical reaction of turning resources into a product. Counterproductive culture as an inhibitor makes seamless production unreachable and utilization of resources costly and inefficient.

Innovation stalls, and human resource turnover is dangerously high, leading to increased labor costs. In simple words, can we make a cup of coffee if we have water and a kettle but no heat source?

Shareholders reasonably and rightfully demand profit from an active organization. In this context, an underperforming company is forced to show unrealistic results by massaging figures on the balance sheet in order to prop up share value and justify bonuses. However, the repeated massaging of figures will lead to a dramatic collapse sooner or later.

Rumors about unfriendly company culture go viral through gossip, internet ratings, and media reports. Recruiting top talent becomes difficult as professionals are not keen to be associated with such an organization. There is no secret that people tend to work much longer for a company which places an emphasis on interpersonal relationships in addition to the value of work tasks.

Dark Kingdom Hostages

A gem shines only if polished with care and love. Human qualities as resources shine the brightest only if similarly crafted and cared for. Otherwise, the value of that critical asset remains low, enriching neither the employee nor the company. Positive or productive culture encourages the best human qualities and gives members a sense of being a proud part of a high-culture organizational landmark. Negative or counterproductive culture makes people feel like they are drowning in a swamp of dysfunctional relations, meaningless work, disrespect, and unfair inner competition. The value of people as resource carriers is lost in the Dark Kingdom.

Cultural environment, positive or negative, defines human behavior, and employees must either choose to accept and adapt to it or to leave. Who would choose to remain in a negative culture for a long period of time? Such a person may simply be extremely loyal, even when unmerited, or perhaps someone who does not have much to offer the organization, or someone seeking personal enrichment or sustenance of some kind, but certainly not a professional who values each day of a career.

So, what is the price for those trapped inside the walls of a Dark Kingdom? Leadership and management author Simon Sinek in his *Find Your Way* noted that "working hard for something we don't care about is called stress; working hard for something we love is called passion" (Sinek 2017, 18). There is no reason to care about an organization which acts unfairly towards its own people. Actually, working in an unfriendly, tense environment is a stress in itself. Dark Kingdom employees pay a tremendous price – emotional exhaustion, depression, lowered self-esteem, and little chance for professional development.

Talking with managers from different countries and industries about their experience working in negative cultures, I received many heart-breaking confessions:

> *I did not want to be even loosely associated with this absurdity and left after two months;*
>
> *At least I know now what a medieval feudal era looks like;*
>
> *It is miserable feeling how my self-respect is vanishing each day;*
>
> *Coming home furious every day is too much for me and my family. Enough is enough.*

One of my ex-colleagues colorfully explained her latest work experience the following way:

> *"First excitement of a new role was quickly gone, pushed out by gremlins of personal non-satisfaction and doubts of my job purposefulness."*

It is impossible to be constantly on alert against negative emotions and aggression among colleagues. Instead of standing by a coffee machine, smiling and chatting with colleagues about something positive, people rush into their office cells. The hostile environment of a negative culture greatly distances people from colleagues and clients, giving them a feeling of isolation from others. They are not concentrating on execution of duties or customer satisfaction, but on survival in the company, experiencing little if any chance for enhanced productivity and creativity.

The price which is paid by hostages of a toxic organizational culture is reflected in fatigue, anxiety, frustration, and stress. An emotional and physical exhaustion results from the hassle and pressure of a negative culture which cannot be compensated by job satisfaction at the end of the day. It accumulates day by day, and at its peak can even affect the health of the organization's members.

Counterproductive culture is characterized by meaningless procedures, overwhelming office formalities, and practices which are time consuming and disorientating, all leaving less time for the achievement of daily goals. Anxiety shadows every action, gradually diminishing self-confidence. Frustration about what could happen next is like riding a roller coaster in a dark tunnel.

Accumulated stress potentially leads to the not-easily curable mental condition of depression. This mental problem directly attenuates productivity due to lowered concentration, cognitive abilities, and efficiency. Work-related depression is a much greater issue than a single business problem; depression is costly in terms of national economies. A United States' 2015 study of workplace mental health, shows that depression costs the US economy 210 billion dollars, of which forty-eight to fifty percent is attributable to workplace stress (Cheang 2017). On a global scale, depression and anxiety is estimated to cost the economy approximate $1 trillion per year. These figures are worrying as they are equal to the gross domestic product (GDP) of a small nation.

In the Dark Kingdom, when looking around the office, people cannot see lighthouses of enthusiasm, strongholds of professional attitude, or real performance heroes. It is normal to benchmark your own performance against that of others, and eventually, low performance becomes a norm across the organization. Little value is added, but a lot of harm is done to overall productivity.

It is very difficult to be loyal to several things at the same time. If people are not satisfied in the work place, then they will shift their loyalty to something else, outside the walls of the dark stronghold. Although physically behind the office desk, they are mentally and emotionally somewhere very far away.

Victims Who Pay the Price

I like watching exciting TV programs with fabulous chefs such as Gordon Ramsay (*Kitchen Nightmares*) and Jamie Oliver (*Jamie's Kitchen*). Besides being incredible chefs, they also demonstrate great leadership and culture management qualities. Most of their programs prove that the "wish-to-be-good" restaurants (chefs they are guiding) have a negative culture which destroys its inner core and turns guests and partners away. Even if a chef helps them by revitalizing the menu and re-opening with the involvement of a well-known personality, it takes time for a team to conquer its inability to satisfy the increased flow of guests.

Examples such as the previous fundraising company story or *Kitchen Nightmares* cases demonstrate that customers and partners become victims of a counterproductive culture. Gordon Ramsay teaches restaurant owners that the way to heal a restaurant's culture and return the business to productivity is to place its focus on serving the customers. Customers and partners bring money into a company. They vote with their wallets and are reluctant to trade with a Dark Kingdom market place.

Disrespect and arrogance rule such an organization, leaving no chance to respect those from the outside. In the view of the Dark Kingdom dwellers, customers and partners are annoying intruders who must leave money and go away. They forget that the market place is tightly packed with similar products and services stimulating fierce competition for customers and reliable partners. Customers are not willing to risk their time or money in the hands of unfriendly and unreliable companies. They will shop where a company is focused on the customer. The normal reaction for most people is to distance themselves from negative people and experiences, particularly when handing over their own hard-earned money.

A company with a counterproductive culture is hardly exhibiting operational excellence and consistent product quality. Such a company is not capable of making its partners strong and tends to drag them down to its level of performance. As previously shown, if a charity delegates a fundraising mission to a contractor with a negative culture, it will jeopardize its reputation and reduce further prospects for quality donations. Dealing with a negative company puts profits at great risk due to the high transaction costs caused by an excessive need to control everything and uncertainty regarding the partner's behavior.

Dark Kingdoms feel little psychological responsibility for their partners' needs and demands; they tend to blame others for their own faults and misconduct. They are not good at helping partners to prosper, but very good at helping partners to falter. Underperforming and badly behaving partners cause risk to a business's success.

Not a Verdict but a Diagnosis

Negative culture is centered on the bosses' ambitions or manipulated by groups of short-sighted managers exercising their hierarchical rights and hiding their uselessness behind false reports. As a result, organizational culture becomes wrongly-focused or neglected completely. If culture is not centered on the people involved with the organization, then it will be a force against the organization. Sick ambitions only call more gremlins into the company, placing goals beyond reach. Difficult or negative emotions build up, mirroring the everyday suffering of employees, and culture becomes toxic. The spectrogram of such companies shows only different shades of grey.

You will not see a polished plaque bearing the name "Dark Kingdom" on the doors of companies with counterproductive cultures. However, there are several clues that help you to recognize them. The most obvious sign is that the company lacks a vital ingredient: a personal touch in organizational life, in its products or services. All effort is directed towards meaningless reports and long presentations which incorporate figures but not the real people behind them. The value of people is not paramount, concentrating instead on orders from management and producing attractive reports.

Other clues include:

- A culture's functions are not harnessed, instead all human processes are regulated artificially from the top;

- You are not welcomed with sincere smiles but instead weighed in terms of status and whether or not you may potentially be a source of future trouble;
- People are in a bad mood most of the time;
- Action means panic as everyone knows how to manage, but not how to do;
- People are fragmented into small non-cohesive cohorts erecting figurative walls of protection around themselves;
- The organization is static, and there are no real signs of change, only a lot of talking about it.

Negative culture drastically damages the other four core systems which form the central nervous system of all organizations – cognition, control, communication, and learning. These systems define an organization's capacity to successfully profit from the exploitation of resources available, react to external changes, secure development, and generate superior knowledge. In simple words, counterproductive culture paralyzes the whole organizational body and restricts growth and market adaptability.

You possibly remember the famous dialogue between Alice and the Cheshire Cat in *Alice in Wonderland.*

"But I don't want to go among mad people," Alice remarked.

"Oh, you can't help that," said the Cat, "we are all mad here. I'm mad. You're mad."

"How do you know I'm mad?" said Alice.

"You must be," said the Cat, "or you wouldn't come here."

Business is a bit of madness considering that it is necessary to satisfy a tremendous number of people and consider an infinite number of issues. My aim is not to judge anyone by pointing out Dark Kingdoms on a map, but to help turn culture into a positive, progressive force, supporting development for years ahead. No one is perfect, but those who build up their inner strength always win. Even Dark Kingdoms have a chance to turn their negative character around and become winners. The first achievement is to recognize the problem.

The opportunity to make your organization stronger is in your hands – recognize problems, implement appropriate changes, and keep strong. For those who think progressively, this is not a verdict, but a call to action.

CHAPTER THREE

SYMBOLS, VALUES, RULES, AND ATTRIBUTES

We can measure physical strength using simple and straightforward methods and metrics. We can measure organizational performance, process efficiency, and outcomes where all these parameters are characterized by the cost and quality of a final product, whether it is something tangible such as a car or sofa, or intangible such as quality of service.

Organizational culture is something that goes beyond simple metrics and common definitions. Thus, understanding it demands the employment of a somewhat metaphysical view - a philosophical explanation of this phenomenon which is embedded in our minds and souls. Culture is made up of our collective endeavors, commitments, emotions, practices, and expectations, and thus is dynamic and complex. Individual views on culture can be very different, but in the back of our minds we know that first of all, culture reflects common values. However, people tend to shade this obvious fact, concentrating on attributes that more easily attract their attention. Is this an inevitable human mistake or a wrongly defined approach to culture management?

Can we precisely measure such human emotions and senses as commitment, effort, respect, loyalty, or satisfaction? The answer is "no." However, we can manage the firm's inner psychological state if we know how to influence values and beliefs. For sophisticated culture management, we need to understand the very nature of culture.

Culture is a hierarchy of strands with symbols at the top and trustworthy cultural signs and attributes at the bottom. It defines the area of an organization's influence and its psychological dimensions where boundaries are signposted by symbols and its inner life is defined by cultural values. Rules function as guidelines which provide a detailed explanation as to the appropriate behavior in different situations. Signs and attributes aid in understanding an organization's culture as a system.

Symbols

It is not always easy to grasp the motivating principle of any organization. Knowing this, we tend to look for symbols to help us understand what defines the inner life of an organization and encourages its people to be proud members. A corporation's symbols are visible from the outside and thus are the first indicators we see. They provoke and form our assumptions about the corporation's inner values, accepted norms of behavior, interaction with procedures, and traditions.

What are symbols? Practically everything can be considered as a symbol as soon as it signifies something greater than itself in that it conveys a deeper meaning to someone. A symbol is a cognitive link between a person and the deep psychological meaning of a concept that exists outside of the person or the symbol itself. An organizational symbol both conveys the central motivating principle of the organization and inspires its members in the pursuit of the organization's goals.

The most well-known symbols are religious or national in nature. The cross is the symbol for all Christians; the star and crescent for Islam, or a flag for a nation. In corporate terms, the Starbucks teams, in their distinctive green and black uniforms, have become a symbol for a culture which unites lovers of the best coffee across the globe. Documents also act as symbols. A nation's constitution, for example, represents the soul of the country and the intentions of its founders. The original copies of such documents are normally considered to be priceless treasures and are guarded as heavily as their nation's leaders.

By forming invisible ties between people and the organization they represent, symbols provide immediate recognition and allow others to understand the values and qualities exercised by the members of the organization. Any organization has a symbolic nature itself whereby the symbol provides a basic perspective of it, anchoring such rational aspects as strategy, management principles, structures, concepts, and development plans through the shared meanings of the organization's members. Thus, symbols are objective in terms of strategic planning and management.

One of the most important roles for a symbol is to function as a unifying force between an organization's members, allowing them to feel that they are part of something big and share a common purpose. Symbols are unique for every state or organization and work as a bridge between present and future. They stimulate active doing (praxis) and reflect the dynamic nature of an organization.

If symbols are abstract and static, this is a very threatening sign which in medical terms is called the "Hypocrite's mask," i.e. a pre-death mask. By looking at an organization's symbols, newcomers can realize how they can accommodate themselves into its culture and how smoothly they can adapt to its inner social life and processes.

Symbols are always unique and specific, being a visible part of culture, whereas values are more the invisible elements of culture. Symbols emphasize an organization's future by promoting and reinforcing a certain social order which will remain constant for years. Thus, symbols are an important part of any organization's long-term strategy.

Values

People prefer to concentrate on things which are visible, although the real strength of a company comes not from a production line but from its culture and values. These intangibles, and the degree to which the organization adheres to them, are far more important than material resources and products.

People talk about values every day. For instance, people hear in conversations: "We value support in on our company," or "We are all as one family." Values regulate behavior and attitudes towards others, and reflect the way people should act, making the organization live and dynamic. A cultural value can be viewed as a broad tendency to prefer certain states of affairs over others (Hofstede 1980, 19). Cultural value reflects how people see relationships and their personal role and feelings in them, whether in the context of organizational or social life.

Values are the pillars that hold up the culture and form the cultural codes which regulate all the unwritten procedures and social norms inside an organization, whether formal or informal.

Values keep an organization's spirit strong and concentrated, defining the organizational conciseness. An organization without prominent cultural values is like a drunk who has lost his way in a blizzard without hope of rescue.

Values define and guide both hierarchical and peer-to-peer relationships. They determine if an organization will be a strong whole or a bunch of separated units. Starbucks Coffee Company is probably the best example of an inclusive and supportive teams' culture. The strong Starbucks' culture is built around four core values - valuing employees and their contributions; close bonds among employees; culture of inclusion and diversity; and taking pride in providing exceptional customer service. The people-centered concept called "return for happiness" has proven to be very effective in terms of Starbucks' growth and success. Starbucks' teams provide competitive advantages to the firm by their ability to attract customers into their warm and cozy cafés.

Real values are transcendent, encouraging people to act for things beyond themselves. Values are signs of good social practice in an organization and reflect human activities and desires - stability, harmony, order, intellectual and effective autonomy, security, quantitative and qualitative growth, fairness, and honesty - i.e. everything that provides self-reflection to employees as valuable and nurtured parts of a firm.

Values define the rationality of irrational choices. People are too rational to jump over limits without strong reasons and financial rewards are not always the best motivators. Clearly and fairly articulated values stimulate people to perform naturally and go that extra mile beyond their normal duties. For instance, people will not usually exhibit a virtue such as bravery solely for financial compensation. However, they will exhibit such virtues in service of causes greater than themselves, such as the many who serve in the military, first responders, and other organizations serving others.

The aim of cultural values is to stimulate employees and encourage a willingness to commit their capabilities to the achievement of an organization's goals. Values which are accepted and supported by members reach their hearts and minds and so allow them to drive an organization beyond rational predictions to reach desired horizons.

It is difficult to expect employees to produce something valuable if their understanding of organizational goals and values does not penetrate down to a gut level. People tend to produce something of quality when it is meaningful to them. If a person's mind is occupied by something of insignificant value, this will most likely be reflected in poor results. In this sense, people will perform only to what is an adequate level of performance and nothing more. Employees will not be prepared to commit their qualities and actions to the highest standards if they don't feel that superior performances are really honored in an organization. Committing oneself to an organization is a long-term obligation and is a critically important decision. It is similar to the commitment necessary to pursue higher education or to become one of the best at a particular sport.

Strategic development reflects an organization's real values and shows how it and its employees will act towards customers and stakeholders. An organization's overall performance is the sum of the performance and input of each employee. If an organization inculcates strong values in its employees, their efforts will combine to ensure success.

Superior financial performance can't be realized without innovativeness, flexibility, and teamwork, which are fostered by core values which define how to treat employees, customers, and other stakeholders. For instance, Citibank is standing strong in many countries by reaffirming values that focus on clients, sustainable shareholders' value, contribution to economic recovery, and "being a bank first." Its program, Responsible Finance, aims to promote a number of initiatives centered on customers and society at large. These initiatives include Supporting Small Business, Communities at Work Fund, Pioneering the Future of Urban Infrastructure, Citi for Cities, Innovating across the Globe and Beyond It, and the Space Shuttle.

In this sense, even such rigid organizations as banks are changing their views on culture implementing different programs in order to reaffirm core values, and aiming to achieve new levels of customer service. For instance, a few years ago Goldman Sachs declared a new approach - not just can they undertake a given business activity, but should they be choosing to concentrate, in every transaction, on the core client service values of integrity, transparency, professional excellence, confidentiality, and respect. Goldman Sachs's declaration states, "Our goals are to maximize individual potential, increase commercial effectiveness, reinforce the firm's culture, expand our people's professional opportunities, and help them contribute positively to their greater communities." In order to strengthen Goldman Sachs' culture, a Business Standards Committee was created in 2010 with a mandate to ensure that the firm's business standards and practices are of the highest quality; that it meets or exceeds the expectations of its clients, other stakeholders, and regulators; and that it contributes to overall financial stability and economic opportunity.

People judge events and actions based on long-standing and trusted values. Conversely, they tend to reject loudly proclaimed "artificial" values which don't appeal to their hearts and minds. A person's decision to accept a job and work for an organization is primarily weighed against their values. Money and promotional chances are important factors, but cultural environment, opportunities for professional and personal achievements, and concern for others often outweigh finances when they accept a job offer.

What is the difference between organizations with a values-centered culture and those with a counterproductive culture? The difference is that leaders of counterproductive organizations are focused on satisfaction of their personal ambitions to the detriment of the organization's people and their interests. If values are not clearly defined, then a control-centered culture, rather than a values-based culture, develops. Instead of encouraging people and driving costs down, the control-based culture makes processes more expensive in terms of both cost and time, and the organization risks falling into the ranks of the Dark Kingdom. From a practical standpoint, the logic is very simple – ignore values and see the capitalization of your company decline, people leave, and customers run to competitors.

Owners and leaders define values in accordance with a vision of their company nature. Thus, culture is always unique as the combinations of values chosen by owners and leaders are endless. A small number of values will be enough to define the core of an organization's culture as soon as they are clearly explained and communicated to employees. Anything more is simply excessive and risks distracting the employees from the things with which they should be concerned.

Rules

What about the written and unwritten rules that exist in every organization? Rules reflect values, oftentimes providing detailed guidelines for people's behavior in various situations. At the same time, rules often develop as a reaction to events in the organization or the wider industry. They express local wisdom, common understanding of what is or isn't acceptable, informal agreements, and as measures against opportunistic behavior.

However, rules cannot provide instructions for every possible situation. Those limitations are transcended by the values that inspired the rules. If an organization does not have firm values and relies merely on rules and codes of employees' behavior, little space is left for ethical decision-making. Corporate codes of ethics become mere words treated as more important than values, resulting in a swamp of formalities and senseless restrictions that weaken a firm from the inside.

When values are not defined, people are left to rely on the rules as a guide. Due to the fact that the rules can't cover every situation, they will multiply, often contradicting each other. This is what happens in counterproductive cultures. Excessive rules leave little chance for developing unofficial but essential relationships and the organization will begin to fragment. Everyone stands individually, rather than collectively, as no force exists to bring people together.

Excessive rules cannot replace values. They only make life inside the organization more complicated and full of traps for the creative people who would normally feed the group's growth. Instead, these people become frustrated and inefficient. This leads to unmanageable formalities and inner bureaucracy, and drives governance and transaction costs higher and higher. Sooner or later, people no longer think of the organization's values as a source of guidance for intra-organizational relationships. They are forced to appeal to rules, reducing opportunities for creativity, and making them skeptical of the honesty and fairness of others. This is like looking for true North using a damaged compass.

No one can get around clearly declared values but there is always a chance to get around or bend the rules, providing a space for opportunistic behavior against the organization, colleagues, or customers.

People use the services of banks, airlines, hotels, utility providers, and others on a daily basis, and I'm sure many of us are well aware of cases in which organizations develop rules that work against basic customer interests. They take relationships with customers for granted, treating customers as some sort of game and ignoring the fact that the organization's existence is at stake. Rules become a hand grenade in incapable hands. It is only a question of how long before it explodes. Therefore, it is imperative to stress that no organization should create rules unknown to customers. Those customers will feel cheated, and opportunistic employees will take advantage of them for their own benefit.

Rules are indispensable instruments but only if they're developed to support cultural values and to help guide people, not to make life in the organization miserable.

Attributes

Willingness to perform comes not from the muscles but from the mind, and performance is possible only if one trusts one's organization and the people in it. Fairness in hierarchical relations, formal and informal roles, and shadow influencers, all affect how people fulfill their obligations and promises towards peers and external stakeholders.

When meeting new people, we are looking for signs to help us judge the environment and determine whether we can trust them and whatever organization they represent. We observe every clue – acts, events, modes of presentation, and everything that allows us to make judgments on whether or not a given culture is trustworthy. We try to understand whether the people we meet are coming from a productive culture or if we are stepping into the swamp of another Dark Kingdom company. Are obligations and promises honored and fulfilled in this company or is it just another 'wish-to-be' scenario?

It is great if trustworthy signs and attributes prove the viability and vitality of declared values and an active inner life is fueling the culture of a given organization. However, values are often replaced by purposeless and meaningless attributes which exist in their own way, i.e. separately from the original goals and values of the organization. In simple words, it is like measuring taste in inches. When this occurs, employees will see the signs and it will affect their work.

What is the difference between real and fake attributes? Let's look at this through the lens of a real case. I was talking with an old gentleman while travelling on a train last year. In the middle of the conversation, he picked up his pocket watch and looked at it. Pocket watches are rarely used today and I was surprised. He looked at the watch differently than a person would check their wristwatch or phone.

I asked him why he used a pocket watch instead of a wristwatch. He replied, "I am old and time is most valuable for me. I consider a standard watch to be an accessory and a pocket watch a kind of time machine, and I use it with great respect."

It was a good lesson as it underscored an understanding of time as having tremendous value. The old man's pocket watch was a tangible symbol that indicated what he valued most. I also know someone who wears a watch which cost as much as a decent house. He is always talking about the importance of time and time management, but he never comes to a meeting on time. In this sense, his watch is only a fancy accessory.

Flashy attributes or accessories cannot stimulate the willingness to perform. Wearing a corporate jacket or badge does not make people better or more persistent, unless they realize the importance of their role for all the organization's members and stakeholders. Fake attributes show that culture is only used as a brainwashing instrument and not a driving force as it is supposed to be. People see this almost immediately and behave accordingly. The costs of implementing meaningless and misleading attributes are wasted without any return. The costs are raised even higher as time goes by as a later realignment of the culture to a more productive state will be both expensive and time consuming.

Noisy events meant to boost morale attract attention, but only for a short while, whereas quiet and consistently strong processes open people's hearts and inspire a desire to be involved. Fake attributes reflect an attitude that treats goods, products, and rituals as things to be manipulated. Real and trustworthy signs work in a positive culture as bridges between hearts and core values, bringing people together in a natural synthesis.

Discussion

An organization's culture informs its members of the behavior which is most appropriate for certain environmental conditions, and by doing so, allows people to achieve their goals. Thus, culture is accountable for achieving a certain level of excellence in living and development. In terms of governance and people management, culture is responsible for influencing people, attuning their minds to shared visions, goals, and appropriate actions. This positive influence can only be gained through the prominent roles of symbols and values.

Cultural hierarchy should be created and maintained from the top to the bottom. Trying to build culture from the bottom upward with mere attributes and rules is like chasing a rainbow to find where it begins and ends. Seasoned leaders are well aware that symbols and values are important for employees, while rules and attributes are praised by those who like jumping between jobs.

More rigorously, symbols and values are associated with employees' reflexive receptiveness of culture and actions evoked by values. By contrast, rules and attributes are associated with the control of behavior. People-centered management as a property of the Knowledge Era is focused on symbols and values aiming to evoke the best people's qualities in service to the organization. Metaphorically speaking, values have a green color as something life-giving, whereas rules are red, functioning as restricting flag posts. Therefore, the goal of value-centered management is to expose human potential.

Imagine a sign on the coat of arms of a nobleman. It is usually written in Latin and depicts core values of the family such as pride, honor, and wisdom. The same sign proclaiming values can be imagined on a company logo. It will be appealing to customers and make employees proud of their involvement.

Building an elegant and solid culture is the pinnacle of the art of leadership. All four critical forces must be prominent, effective, and working towards cultural enhancement. Symbols, values, rules, and attributes are interdependent and work effectively only if well-defined and supportive of each other. Delete or ignore one of these forces and the culture will collapse, burying the whole organization. If rules and attributes prevail over values and symbols, then expect a negative culture to flourish, turning a once great organization into another Dark Kingdom, unable to satisfy owners or employees.

Practical Tips:

- Chose three to five core values reflecting vision and evoking the best human qualities needed for achievement of your organization's goals. Three is a minimum number of values needed to support employees' psychological aims. At the same time, people will lose focus if more than five values are declared.

- Your organization's values should echo human values and desires, otherwise they will be meaningless.

- An ability to translate values into practice and reality matters most. Simple declaration of values without actions is self-defeating.

- Your organization's purpose and goals must be aligned with values that allow for the control of actions and the ability to benchmark stages of development against them.

- If rules are not in line with values, then they simply imitate natural control and care of people. Massaging rules for the sake of changing them leads to chaos and misalignment of values.

- If culture turns negative, look at whether or not your rules and attributes support your organizational core values.

- Values are important for believers and rules are praised by manipulators.

- Values are not patterned statements, but have a tacit nature because an advanced understanding of them is born among employees. Only then are they fully visible to external stakeholders. Thus, let employees get involved in discussing them.

- The result of your organization's activity reflects what is proclaimed most in the company. For instance, if values are regarded most highly, then profit results from the increased performance of loyal employees and a growing number of satisfied customers, i.e. qualitative growth. If rules are praised above all, then the outcomes will reflect a growing number of employees with average performance levels and increasing governance costs, i.e. quantitative growth.

CHAPTER FOUR

ENERGY SOURCES

Culture as Energy

Culture provides an inner psychological energy to an organization and instills a sense of purpose. The Ancient Greeks viewed energy (*energia* – old Greek) as activity or the capacity to do work.

Energy can't be utilized separate from an external, physical source. We see energy not only in individuals but in teams as well. While watching a boring football game, we may comment that there is no energy in the teams. The same can be said about organizations of any size, from small businesses to large corporations; in all of them, maintaining a strong inner source of energy is a matter of life and death.

To understand organizational energy we may look at it as a sophisticated system. In this sense, energy can be positive or negative depending on whether it drives an organization forward or holds it back. An organization's energy system represents an interdependent composition of factors shaped and bounded by that organization's culture. This human-made system, created by people and for people, does not allow for ill-conceived manipulation and takes into account the influence of factors like the environment and stakeholders of many kinds.

It is necessary to monitor the group's energy to ensure that it remains compatible with the organization's goals, strategic plans, and actual purpose of its existence. This is like reading and reacting to data from a flight recorder on an everyday basis, rather than waiting until after an accident happens. If we want to fly higher, then we must keep the energy high and positive while remaining attentive to all the relevant factors. The management of the positive emotional and psychological energy of an organization is a daily task of every leader and manager.

Culture as Energy of Many

The roots of cultural energy lie deep in the beliefs, desires, concerns, and inner reflections of every employee. The combined energy of people who are gathered in the name of achieving the same goals is a tremendous force. Combined together it can defeat obstacles. The only questions are: What is nature of this energy? Where is it directed? What factors contributes to a positive or negative culture?

Sources of Positive Energy

Many factors influence the nature of the energy and cultural climate inside a company. Here, we will limit ourselves to the seven most critical factors – respect, job satisfaction, involvement, loyalty, shared affection and support, preparedness for change, and responsibility. We will spend time looking at the factors influencing a negative culture.

Respect and Self-Respect

We respect those who respect us. As applied to organizations, people will not commit their best endeavors to a company which is disrespectful to its employees. Why should people share their best qualities knowing that they wouldn't be valued? Respect is a give and take relationship working on all organizational levels – between colleagues, in relations between supervisors and subordinates; essentially, in all hierarchical relations.

It begins with the respect shown in hierarchical relations. This has remained unchanged for centuries. Sun Tzu in his *The Art of War* (Part 10.25) viewed respect as an important feature of success: "Regard your soldiers as your children, and they will follow you into the deepest valleys; look on them as your own beloved sons, and they will stand by you even into death." If employees feel respected and appreciated, they become more loyal, feeling obliged to work effectively while actively engaged in company life.

Respect can't be won by cheap words, nice presentations, and speeches, but rather is gained incrementally, day by day. This creates genuine excitement in working for a company, pride for one's work, and respect among peers and superiors, which in turn creates and responds to human energy. Trust, teamwork, and shared visions can't be developed without respect incorporated into internal relationships.

Real respect in an organization can be weighed against a strongly neglected factor, the self-respect of employees.

When talking to one of my contacts about how he felt as part of a well-known international company, I got a striking response:

"I hate myself for working for company X. I am losing self-respect and belief in my skills and feel I am gradually hiding from any responsibilities and duties. It looks like I lost everything I was good at before. I'm not the only one who feels that way. No money can compensate for this."

Lately, I have come across a huge number of similar responses from adults who feel trapped in a Dark Kingdom organization. A modern problem is that too many people, even those involved in decision-making, have similar experiences which negatively shape their professional lives. Where do these emotions come from? Commonly, this negative slide begins by incidents of management blaming others and threatening subordinates which eventually grow into standard practice and begin ruining a company from the inside.

The answer to a simple question - "Am I proud of myself or do I dislike myself?"- is a good indicator of how things are going in your own organization. How would your employees answer this question? How far can an organization go if just one-third of its people have a feeling of self-loathing? In this case, owners pay dearly for it as the organization's performance begins to degrade.

Job Satisfaction

Skills enhancement and knowledge acquisition are natural goals for most people as it provides them with a sense of self-satisfaction and confidence in the future. We understand intuitively that if we are not growing, then we are falling behind while others are achieving better competencies and, consequently, advancing their careers. The kind of self-motivated people that grow an organization also feel the need to personally grow professionally on a daily basis.

It is true that on one hand, people fear change and crave stability. On the other, we also understand that if our skills and competencies are not improving, they are falling behind in today's dynamic marketplace.

As one manager admitted:

"A feeling of professional satisfaction when doing good work is the best reward I can get from my company. This is an invaluable feeling; almost like a drug because I want more and more of it. This is "Ode to Joy" inside me telling me that I did my best and I am proud of it."

The excitement of continually augmenting one's performance instills the type of confidence that can be seen in the eyes of seasoned professionals. One confident professional is better than three hesitant ones. Individuals lacking in confidence, though often flashy with the perceived ability to always seem to know what to say, often don't know the taste of real achievement and would not fight for it, instead seemingly expecting employers to cherish them just for their presence in an office.

High organizational performance requires a high quality effort from every employee and good people don't come cheap. People want to be valued in the job market, both for their personal satisfaction and so they can provide for their families.

Inadequate compensation leads to personnel believing they are undervalued by one's organization and causes people to find a place where they will be valued appropriately.

A business development manager for a food distribution company remarked:

> *"My company is showing greater profit every year but pay is only rising by a tiny percentage to compensate inflation. How come the profits of my work are escalating, but my value to the company is not growing? Or perhaps even declining? It has happened for a few years in a row and now I feel I have lost years of my professional life. I can't tell my wife that instead of an appropriate pay raise I am getting a pat on the shoulder. I don't see a reason to push myself anymore. Let it be the boss's problem. I'll be looking for a better opportunity with competitors."*

Requiring employees to work harder to compensate for the poor performance of others, while being compensated equally with them, is a drastically unsuitable approach with deleterious consequences. This is tantamount to a communist system of even distribution without regard to individual input and its results. These systems have universally led nowhere but to unhappy people and weak economies.

Professional and financial growth goes hand in hand with the psychological. One person may accept a job offer expecting to grow professionally, while another aims simply to make money. Real personal satisfaction, however, comes when both are secured, leaving the only acceptable reason for being unsatisfied as one's craving for personal growth. Any organization that takes its people seriously will strive to provide avenues for members to satisfy those cravings. The organization with such a culture becomes a source of pride for employees and employers alike.

Enthusiasm, inspiration, and passion are the result of employees' job satisfaction fueling an organization's growth. Satisfied people spread this feeling around them and, as a result, influence others to greater levels of achievement. However, the opposite feeling of non-satisfaction goes viral among colleagues as well, creating a deep-seated pessimism, a distinctive feature of a Dark Kingdom organization.

Involvement

We feel involved in systems that we can change over time, either short or long, hopefully in a positive way. People don't feel involved if they can't change things for the better. Even doing the same task every day for many years gives a sense of involvement as soon as it is reflected in something important. This self-perception of being a part of something important makes fulfilling one's duties deeper than simply following an operations manual. A feeling of involvement grows with a better understanding of one's own role in the achievement of greater goals. An inadequately understood goal in the employee's personal view diminishes the involvement.

Those employees who are really involved tend to question themselves: What is my personal mission in this organization? How can I accomplish it? Proper involvement is worrying about how the result of your work is echoing in the feelings of a customer on the other side of the world. Being drawn into the listlessness presented in negative cultures, employees quickly lose a sense of involvement, even those who are self-motivated.

The 2017 Gallup Employee Engagement report (Crabtree 2017) shows that only fifteen percent of employees are actually engaged in the work process. Having more people really involved can ultimately increase positive outcomes. Considering the importance of involvement, it must be managed on an individual level daily and not by declaring ad hoc campaigns.

A desire to leave, whether to wait for a genuinely better opportunity or to simply leave at the first opportunity, has a huge effect on people's expended efforts. Looking for an opportunity in the outside world is like having one hand occupied with a packed suitcase and attention split between the current task and checking out the job boards. There is little involvement, little desire to improve performance, and not much interest in anything going on at work. Most of what a person in that situation is thinking about it is the potential of something else.

One of my respondents confessed, that:

"I used to work for a yacht building company and loved those snow-white beauties. One day the company was sold and new owners hired migrants to do a majority of the work, i.e. guys who worked for a few months and were gone. Those beauties meant nothing to them; traditions are meaningless in their view; work is just a necessary evil. Soon, an atmosphere of indifference conquered the yard. Yachts were still shiny but I know that actual quality has gone down dramatically. The veterans became treated similar to those one-week cowboys. I lost this special sense of being part of something important and left the company."

In simple words, involvement is not merely an attachment or association. It is the difference between employees believing they can make a difference or believing they are nothing more than a replaceable cog in a machine.

People become loyal when a company's values and goals line up with their own and they feel their contributions are valued. In organizational terms, loyal employees are those insiders who see the big picture, are confident about an organization's stability and potential, and sacrifice even when there are drawbacks. Loyalty is not simply blind. Good employees are aware of different negative issues which can be seen in any company.

Loyalty fills the relationship between employer and employee with meaning. Otherwise, an employee becomes just a paid temporary laborer and not a valuable part of the organization. This is similar to mercenaries that don't care about whatever cause they are fighting for; they are loyal only to themselves. Thus, being loyal means caring about an organization, approaching work with a firm sense of commitment, and consequently the organization has an obligation to reciprocate that treatment. Appreciation of employees' loyalty is tremendously important but doesn't demand much effort. Honest feedback and a word of appreciation make a huge difference.

Unfortunately organizations often exploit their employees, taking loyalty for granted. They push people beyond sensible limits and thus sabotage that loyalty. Don't kill the motivation of those doing their best. In such cases, employees are not only pushed to their limits but to the exit. With them goes their years of accumulated experience and storehouse of knowledge.

How would you value, in monetary terms, a loyal employee vs. one that is not deemed loyal? Of course, it is impossible to calculate the effect of loyalty precisely but we can use common sense and understand the difference it makes to have friends or supporters inside your business. Lack of loyalty or a loss of it has an undeniable corrosive effect and rots an organization from the inside. The ripple effect from this hurts customers and partners who will then seek for solutions elsewhere, hastening the organization's death spiral. The reason is simple: customers' loyalty begins with the loyalty of employees. Loyal employees are necessary to create loyal customers. But, non-loyal employees are more likely to upset even existing customers. Very logically, if staff is not loyal to the organization, they will not be likely to treat its customers well or may speak ill of the organization. Loyal employees consider customers as the most valuable asset of their organization and care about them accordingly, whereas those who are not loyal look at customers as obstacles to a laid-back and easy life.

Another extreme comes in the form of people who change jobs frequently, often within a year or two. They don't even have time to become loyal. They are not worried about customers or productive inner relationships but only nice additions to their CV. Unfortunately, those "experts" in Human Resource Management (HRM), who are supposed to think about their organization's growth, are busily writing in almost every article that modern managers should be jumping between jobs. This is strange advice, as one doesn't have the opportunity to build experience, thus harming companies by perpetuating a lack of competent employees. Instead of praising people who have worked for one organization for many years and have a true sense of loyalty, a dangerous trend of devaluing such people in favor of hyper-mobility has developed.

Shared Affection and Support

A ship can't up anchor and proceed to the high seas without the crew, shoulder to shoulder, pulling ropes together and being prepared to withstand potentially severe storms. If we win, we win together. As people in such situations grow together, learn from each other, and support each other, a shared affection develops.

It is difficult for an organization to prosper without those kinds of strong inner relationships that develop in a positive culture. An advanced tacit knowledge, mutual intuition, enhanced integrity, and simultaneous effort can't be realized without shared affection and mutual support. Shared affection further builds workplace friendships and increases support among colleagues, which leads to employees' positive attitudes, improved resilience to stressors, and highly valued reciprocity.

People concentrate on achieving a goal and not on meaningless gossip. They focus on priorities. There is no tolerance for wasting the time and effort of others in such an environment. Certainly, colleagues may have hot disputes about the rationality of particular processes or the best ways of doing things; however, shared affection ultimately reduces aggression and helps to avoid workplace conflicts. The focus is shifted from personal ambitions and egoistic points to task fulfillment and improvement.

Organizations function best when inner relations are productive, and people feel useful to the group and receive emotional support from peers. This is like a family environment where members are concerned about one other, support each other, and have similar goals. This helps to close the gap between work duties and social life making life less contradictory and more organic. This is altruism in its best form, doing good for one's self and with a great use for others as well.

Shared affection reveals hidden personal qualities and a desire to help others, adding a great deal of energy into the working environment. The work place becomes fun, enthusiastic, and appealing when people love to be there. Allow people to feel important to and to be supported by their peers, and management and performance will necessarily improve.

Preparedness to Change

The vast majority of people are not eager to leave their comfort zone, the cozy little bubble where they know every little thing. I know a ship's chief engineer who worked on the same boat for thirty years. He claims to be an expert but the problem is that he will not be as good on another ship, particularly during a fleet upgrade. Everything tends to change, and often the environment changes at enormous speed and those things which were advanced a few months ago are becoming dated as we speak.

Capacity for change is determined by very personal indicators like inner strength, the desire to be better than somebody else; one's own ambitions; and a number of other internal factors. It is a matter of realizing who you want to be after going through a change.

From a purely professional standpoint, preparedness to change is triggered by a competition against company and industry experts. How others change and grow professionally is a very important factor which employees need to see clearly.

Preparedness to change defines people's adaptability to progress. An organization's ability to change comes from the combined preparedness for change of every individual. Coping with change is the result of learning, whether from experience or formal education. Thus, a conscious willingness to learn contributes to preparedness for change. Also, in some professions learning and preparedness to change is driven by the job itself, as is the case with pilots or software engineers, where preparedness to change is imprinted in their minds. For others it is a market condition where preparedness to change is more of a personal initiative in order to catch up with the latest trends. Thus, it is important from whom we learn, whether from those respected in our organization or industry, or from someone conducting a brainwashing session presented by a strange business coach talking about the same irrelevant platitudes over and over again.

Most people have some innate desire to learn and explore but also realize that it isn't achieved without cost, demanding effort, time, and resources. Once started, it is an endless process. Contrary to positive companies, Dark Kingdom organizations are not prepared to cover the high costs for mature mentors to support the ambitions of those wishing to learn, unless mandated by the industry's regulations. Thus, their employees' preparedness to change inevitably drains out. This is a disastrous property of a counterproductive culture.

Responsibility

My friend has had a Singer sewing machine in his family for few generations. The machine was made in 1920 and is still functioning well. The manual states: "Your children will enjoy using our faultless sewing machine 50 years from purchase date. Signed by X." This is the personal responsibility of someone who thoroughly checked every little thing and gave promises on behalf of the manufacturer.

Responsibility is an authentic mark of quality, one that needs to be consistently exhibited in all aspects of work. A high sense of responsibility means high quality; low responsibility means bad or inconsistent quality. People who feel responsible don't ruin an organization or its reputation but act with integrity and purpose, even at great cost to themselves.

Premier league football teams are different from those from a second division because of the responsibility taken by each player in every win or loss. Responsibility is the basis of an organization's accountability, a critical feature of a sustainable organization. It can't be the responsibility of a few but requires everyone involved. Realizing and fulfilling an organization's and the customers' demands, and keeping standards high, are the result of responsibility. Nobody is perfect and mistakes are inevitable, however, if a mistake is made, responsible individuals are prepared to admit fault and correct it without delay.

Responsibility can be viewed from two separate perspectives. Responsibility consists of performing duties without supervision, or being in charge of a task and being held accountable for the results. Operating like this is necessary for an efficient organization. It shows a level of trust, increases employee morale, and allows for lower costs overall. In collective terms, one can concentrate on the execution of tasks by relying on colleagues without looking over one's own shoulder or that of their colleagues.

Responsibility is also a reflection of self-discipline and keeps people motivated to keep pushing themselves.

It is pointless to anticipate good results from those with little sense of responsibility. Identify the employees trying to escape from responsibilities and you will know where to expect poor results. Unless those who are not very responsible by nature are aware of possible punishment for poor performance they can be counted on to do their job poorly.

Responsibility also means being aware of unrealistic demands and recognizing the line between doing and promising. Unrealistic promises are a form of dishonesty which is the opposite of responsibility. Irresponsible people have difficulties recognizing sensible limits and damage the group's reputation as well as their own. They are lying to themselves and to the organization, which leads to illusive performance and real loses. Look at board meetings in the Dark Kingdom company – too many promises show that not much will actually be accomplished and little responsibility will be assumed.

Energy Killers or Negative Factors

Life is not simple and no one promised that it would always be bright and easy. Unfortunately, there are always negative forces ready to disrupt a positive culture. Again, they are the result of human intentions and behaviors which are disastrous for organizational culture.

Dishonesty

An atmosphere of dishonesty is often palpable and will eventually be recognized by external stakeholders. It causes an avalanche of letters, reports, and emails of complaints, which are often ignored. Dishonesty is a human characteristic which spreads as water ripples if tolerated by an organization's leadership. There is little chance to build a strong productive culture in such an organization, unless it is fully overhauled and the epicenters of such dishonesty (i.e. the people involved) are dealt with.

Don't foolishly expect dishonest people who are not performing well with small tasks to successfully complete a complicated task. "Whoever is faithful in small matters will be faithful in large ones; whoever is dishonest in small matters will be dishonest in large ones. If then, you have not been faithful in handling worldly wealth, how can you be trusted with true wealth?" (The Holy Bible 1992, Luke 16:10-11).

It is very easy to spot an organization which is rotten with dishonesty. Presumably, they don't believe, or even recognize, their dishonesty, and often posters and emails proclaiming their "honesty" are pervasive. This is like a pirate flag waving on the mast of a Dark Kingdom organization.

Jerky Pattern of Decision Making

Frequent and abrupt changes in decisions can destabilize even calm people resulting in unfocused individuals who are often left confused with no idea what to do. Thus, indecisive and reactionary management is an enemy of loyalty, responsibility, involvement, and shared affection. People get exhausted feeling like they are facing a wild fire every day. They lose faith in the organization, have little understanding what their role is, and don't want to be involved in such a mess.

As one of my respondents said:

"Don't rush to do your job, things may change by evening."

Such an environment creates a culture of indecisiveness and procrastination. Employees have nothing on which to direct their focus and become demotivated by the culture.

Working without purpose is like looking for something in the dark without knowing what you're looking for. Motivation and enthusiasm easily become lost resulting in a group of people who work only for the paycheck. Employees see little chance for using their talents or are continually given tasks beyond their competence.

There is no chance to develop shared affection and genuine involvement when the goals are unclear. Unclear goals beget disappointment and burnout, leaving people wondering for what they had worked so hard. Having a clear goal allows employees to focus their energy. Therefore, if an organization doesn't have a clear goal, there is nothing for employees to rally around besides a payday.

Not Valuing People

Employees are not an eternally renewable resource which can be exploited irresponsibly. Unfortunately, some companies don't recognize this. A dreadful atmosphere of arrogance, distrust, and disrespect turns professionals away and only those desperate for employment will work there and then only for as long as necessary. If not valued, they will leave, causing high turnover with no chance for loyalty and involvement resulting in higher costs in recruitment and training. Who wants to be used? Exploiting and devaluing people are sure paths to destroying an organization. The way people are treated in such an organization is the best indicator of how deeply it has gone into Dark Kingdom territory.

It may sound like something from the Bronze Age but many such organizations do exist. In practice, these companies are harming markets and people's lives wherever they operate, whether in advanced or in emerging economies.

Lack of Authenticity

Authenticity forms the core of understanding how we interact with others. It demands we interact with others honestly. We expect others to be genuine; however, with a lack of authenticity on our own part, geniality disappears.

It is natural for people to respect hierarchy, tolerate pressure from leaders, and resist negative events, as these norms are inherent in human nature. Lack of authenticity causes struggles as employees experience cognitive dissonance, and lose a sense of themselves. Restoring authenticity is a tough challenge not everyone will embrace.

Sick Ambitions

Excessive ambitions lead to unrealistic demands, creating discontented employees who are unhappy and likely to lash out.

A department head in a big international company shared his experience:

"I don't want to work with someone with excessive ambitions. He predictably blames others for his faults, has a repugnance and fear of working together, and destabilizes me each time we work together. I do not envy his subordinates."

Excessive and misplaced ambitions cause power struggles because such people are not prepared for the compromise or decisions necessary to achieve the mutual goals of the company. They are only interested in their own desires. One such person can effectively block the functioning of an entire department and the higher the rank of the individual, the greater the damage to the organization will be. Everyone has seen similar cases but do not always realize the dramatic consequences for the organization.

Work-Life Balance

The recent adoption of the term "work-life balance" is a misleading buzzword that is doing more harm than good. It is a complete inversion of most people's priorities. People work for their families; they do not have families for work. Their families deserve time and attention and it is not for the employer to decide how much time one should devote to the family outside of normal office hours. Motivation and involvement disappears when the family begins to suffer because the mother or father continually comes home late and is always stressed out. The results are predictable.

Discussion

It is impossible to pull a rabbit out of a hat if it has no rabbit in it. If employers want positive input from their employees they must take care of them, treating them as valued members of the organization. Otherwise, they will pull out a nasty cold-blooded snake instead of the energized rabbit. In terms of culture, we get out what we put into it.

Relying on external resources and maintaining a lean organization is not enough to ensure long-term success. Mobilizing one's own inner resources consistently leads to sustainable development and competitiveness in the long run. Respect, engagement, and shared affection are not guaranteed or included as part of an employment contract, but instead spring from the company's culture. That culture is largely influenced by the way employers treat their employees. Employers need to earn respect and engagement every day, drop by drop; and they can lose it all in one moment if not careful. Therefore, this should be incorporated into the way managers treat each other, their stakeholders, and employees every day.

Practical Tips

- A gem doesn't shine in darkness and people are no different. People often need the help of their organization to shine. Help them if you want to succeed.

- There is a natural human craving to be part of something bigger than oneself; to fulfill a purpose, be a part of an organization, or to be a citizen of a country. Letting employees be passionate about their duties engages their talents to the fullest and causes them to feel like an integral part of the organization. Otherwise, they will find a better place for their talents and qualities, most likely with your competitors.

- Having more people really involved in an organization can ultimately increase organizational performance. However, it must be managed individually.

- There are always doubters and haters in any organization. They see the glass as half-empty or even spit poison into it. Lose them immediately before they further damage the culture.

- Value people not by their words but by their effort and you will not be disappointed.

- Look at sources of positive energy as indispensable properties of success. Top-off the energy reservoir daily, purify if it turns negative, and keep it refreshed.

- Organizations pay a hefty price for the increased stress and demotivation of employees in terms of decreased profits.

- Stimulation of negative or misleading factors leads to nurturing a counterproductive culture and pushing an organization into an abyss of underperformance.

CHAPTER FIVE

METAPHYSICAL RESOURCES

Energy Reservoirs

Millions of small streams make forceful rivers that feed lakes and oceans. The same principle applies to an organization's energy which comes from the effort and input of every employee who functions as a river supplying the group's energy reservoirs. This supply in turn feeds performance and achievement of the organization's goals. When the employees' motivation is sapped, the rivers are poisoned and the reservoir becomes a swamp.

Employee energy joins together to create more powerful forms of energy through their collective effort. This can't happen without an understanding of the prominent role culture plays in concentrating and directing this energy. Ideally, the culture should encourage every component and factor to add positive energy into the corporate bloodstream to push the business forward. In practice, we understand that there will be negative inputs. It is therefore important that the positive far outweigh the negative.

An organization exists to achieve its goal and provide results which satisfy stakeholders while remaining financially viable. This can be achieved only through consistently improving performance. There are many variables that affect the energy added to an organization - teamwork, professionalism, creativity, accountability, trust, and shared vision. It is important to understand how they operate for the benefit of the organization.

Teamwork

Great results are rarely achieved through the efforts of one sole person. In the vast majority of cases, a team is required. Flying an aircraft, building a house, operating on a patient, most things involve teamwork. A good team is characterized by collaboration, highly developed tacit knowledge, internal discipline, and mutual support. Teamwork is selflessness for the sake of creating something great in cooperation with others who share the same goals.

If cultivated, teamwork has an enormous return on investment for any organization. A company that understands this will undertake efforts to improve the cohesion of their teams. For instance, Southwest Airlines facilitates regular team-oriented trainings that improve the ability of their staff to support and work with each other.

Effective teamwork is built on strong internal ties, mutual support, and shared knowledge. Strong internal relations, not internal competition, make a culture strong. Intense competition may result in accomplished individuals but it will weaken the company's internal relationships, leaving little chance for support and collaboration. Strong internal relationships will also translate into strong external relationships with suppliers and clients.

Humans tend to mimic the actions of those around them, even to the point of walking at the same pace when walking with another. It is important, therefore, that the correct people are teamed with one another. Poor team construction leads to negative synergy, underperformance, and poor customer service. The team becomes a bunch of egocentric individuals without discipline requiring greater amounts of supervision. US Marine Corps General Robert B. Neller stated "Our discipline to orders is what sets us apart." The Marines are renowned for this discipline and commitment to a team's goals.

High staff turnover, inability to recognize the complementary value of each member, and lack of accountability result in low engagement and weak relationships. The subsequent effect on teamwork is devastating, negatively affecting the entire organization.

Innovativeness

Creativity and innovativeness are a necessity for any contemporary company. This means there has to be a willingness to take risks and find new ways of doing things to meet customer demands. Without creativity, a company will soon lose its relevance to the market. Those who challenge the status quo are those who push innovation forward. Icons of product innovation such as Apple and SpaceX readily come to mind. There are also creative approaches to team management and processes in companies like Starbucks, Amazon, or Disney that have made them leaders in their fields and fueled the imagination and efforts of their competitors. Modern business is racing for exceptional products, quality of service, and unique operations and business models that both encourage innovation and lower costs.

If you don't want to see your organization get lost among millions of other dull ventures, then stimulate people to express themselves and be original and you will see them creating tremendous things with others following suit. Developing and nurturing this kind of environment should be a priority for any company.

When developing new technologies, it is important to consider Einstein's quote: "Imagination is more important than knowledge." (Einstein 2009, 97) Creativity often requires that we learn while doing. Refusing to take this chance would mean moving not far, if at all, from where we are now. Thus any company claiming to be progressive must enthusiastically nurture a culture of creativity and innovation.

Let's look at innovativeness from other angle. If no innovation takes place, the organization becomes boring and faceless. People are not robots and it is difficult to expect them to perform at their best if they become bored by the lack of opportunity to push themselves and others. Relieve employees from stifling procedures and excessive formalities and innovativeness will grow, making staff, customers, and owners happy.

The nature of creativity and innovation are such that it is better to encourage than regulate them, which kills them at inception. Unleashing your employees' natural creativity will add fresh energy to the company and allow it to remain competitive as the market continues to change.

Professionalism

Formal management likes talking about productivity as a critical dimension of any organization's existence. This is true. It has to be considered as more than a measure of the profit squeezed from employees vs. their paychecks.

Professionalism comes into play when productivity and innovation have to be maintained over time. Like water persistently cutting through rock, persistence is another name for professionalism and will allow a motivated team to eventually overcome any problem. Is it possible to tell the difference between a culture of productivity and a culture of professionalism? Productivity depends on a set of skills. Professionalism is nurtured within a company and assumes productivity, consistency, the ability to act in different conditions, and attention to detail. Professionalism is accompanied by confidence which is essential for success. In practice, professionalism can't be gained on your own but only in a supportive environment where people learn from others and grow professionally. Dysfunctional teams don't cross rough oceans or climb Everest.

Universities and business schools graduate young people with a high capacity for productivity. However, employers should be more interested in young employees who have been trained to be professionals, who have become not just productive children but responsible adults. A sense of professionalism is what contemporary business truly needs to maintain a positive culture.

For those praising productivity alone, there are side effects to that approach. Productivity is often only a measure of a particular task and doesn't guarantee the same results in the future, especially concerning different tasks that will have to be performed by all of us at some point. Productivity levels often fall with a change of context and circumstances. Professionalism, by contrast, helps a company adapt to and overcome inevitable challenges. Productivity is benchmarked against previous or desired outcomes, whereas professionalism facilitates non-stop appraisal of capabilities and encourages constant learning and improvement.

Accountability

Life, full of mistakes, faulty decisions, and bad circumstances, is never smooth. Moving forward without admitting and correcting mistakes undermines an organization, erodes past successes, and becomes a drag on future efforts. Accountability requires transparency and integrity which is always appreciated by both employees and external stakeholders.

Strong culture requires accountability, i.e. taking responsibility for all actions and events, which is not always easy. Being able to do this is a mark of the strongest character. Those who never admit to their mistakes tend be of weak character, full of pride and fear. Companies with a negative culture often forget the importance of accountability and spend as much time explaining their mistakes as they do trying to reach their goals. The result is a lack of motivation and an increase in cynicism among its employees.

Business is accountable for what it creates and the results of this process. That includes impact on the environment as well as the psychological and financial impact on its employees and the local communities. Employees are more enthusiastic working for a company with clear accountability. Such a company is less likely to blame actions on the lowest level in the employee hierarchy. Blame is assigned where it belongs, no matter how high or low the ranking in the organization. In terms of culture, nothing is more pragmatic than being honest.

Accountability helps to eliminate hidden problems quickly and take appropriate actions to correct them, avoiding the negative consequences of them going undetected. It is very discouraging to realize that an organization has moved in the wrong direction because of an old mistake and learning large amounts of resources have been wasted as a result.

A company's accountability represents its commitment to internal justice and transparency. Thus, accountability can be viewed as a supervisor dedicated to rooting out mistakes and bad behaviors before they become a drag on the whole organization.

Shared Vision

Shared vision exists when a group of people is consciously working toward achieving the same goal. No force is stronger than people united by a common goal; making decisions together and acting as one. Instilling a shared vision is goal prior to profit and is critical for the success of any organization.

An organization's vision belongs to no one person. This is a collective property and is ideally shared by all employees. No company can be successful if a majority of employees doesn't have a clear vision and understanding of where their ship is going. Those who recognize this situation will leave. No one wants to be adrift on a corporate "Flying Dutchman."

A shared vision allows an organization's energy to be focused in one direction toward achieving strategic goals and securing a market leading position for years to come. A recent example is the automotive company Jaguar which lost its prominent market position after being sold to Ford. When it was sold again, its new management instilled a new shared vision in their employees, restoring Jaguar's reputation and position in the market.

People with a shared vision make that vision their own, and don't need to be pushed to do their job. Work becomes more than just a job. It's a matter of personal pride. Shared vision provides a mechanism of self-regulation in an organization, securing greater informal control over actions. In this kind of self-regulating system, behaviors are self-correcting and mistakes detected and corrected early on, resulting in high efficiency and lower costs. In other words, it is functioning as organizational homeostasis in terms of detecting and correcting deviations.

Trust

Trust is a macro-perspective phenomenon which acts as a lubricant for all external and internal processes. Often being irrational, trust is even more valuable than loyalty which has more of calculative nature. It covers all unwritten and unsaid aspects of human interaction and stimulates willingness to collaborate. Trust helps control and directs the various energy streams from different kinds of people.

Trust is a necessity for a high functioning organization. It allows people to work with confidence in their decisions and in those of others. If people can be trusted by their peers and supervisors to do their jobs, they work more efficiently and are happier in their work. One can determine the level of trust that exists in an organization by seeing how they deal with problems. Does the bank teller hesitate to call the manager? When the manager comes out, is he/she impatient or combative with the employee? These interactions reveal a great deal about that institution's character.

Trust is a two-way street. Employees trust their company if it trusts them. If people trust their customers, then more likely customers will trust the organization and the people in it. An organization can't grow without trust from stakeholders and their enthusiastic support as a result of it. Trust grows within an organization among employees and spreads beyond its boundaries, or as far as an organization's culture can reach. People are more willing to invest themselves in an organization if they trust it, and naturally become more engaged as a result.

High performance levels can't be achieved without trust. It reduces transaction and governance costs dramatically, stimulates effective interaction among employees and external stakeholders, and encourages information sharing. Trust is a mark of a risk-free and meaningful relationship, which is critical for non-linear collaboration and achievement of organizational goals. An organization can't sustain itself if trust doesn't exist.

Metaphysical Resources

Each energy component which we discussed above has a direct impact on value creation and the quality of any organization's product and service. They are as valuable as any tangible or intangible resources an organization has.

There is also a third type of resource necessary for value creation in any organization - metaphysical resources.

These metaphysical resources become available to an organization only as a result of positive energy which comes from the positive input and effort of every employee. Metaphysical resources have a large impact on the behavior and performance of employees and shaping the human, social, and economic factors of an organization. Organizations can't exist without effective teamwork, shared vision, advanced professionalism, or prominent trust. Thus, these resources are vital to maintain an organization's existence. It is like a strong family where love and respect are the metaphysical resources necessary for a long and happy marriage.

Why should these metaphysical resources be considered as resources in management terms? There are many critical aspects of the role metaphysical resources play.

A metaphysical resource becomes a resource as a result of an organization's cultural values and the values of employees being aligned. Metaphysical resources also work as a lens enriching and focusing the energy coming from every employee. Metaphysical resources are different from intangible resources. Intangible resources have a formal nature being legally and formally defined, whereas metaphysical resources have a subjective nature being the result of collective input.

Metaphysical resources have a direct impact on value creation and the quality of an organization's inner life. They also form the inner energy field of a company transforming it into an energy-generating body. We can't measure them precisely using conventional metrics, similar to intangible resources. At the same time, these resources have many essential and irreplaceable functions and properties without which no organization can exist. They are essential for attracting customers, satisfying investors, driving development, guaranteeing quality, and securing attractiveness for investors.

They are not directly reflected on a balance sheet but have a direct impact on resources important for an organization's capitalization and thus, either increase or decrease goodwill.

Metaphysical resources have a transformative nature. They can change and can be changed. Like oil, which can be burned for heat or treated to produce plastic, metaphysical resources transform everything with which we interact.

These resources have direct impact on performance and thus, on the results of an organization's activity. Would a company feel the loss if metaphysical resources were not available, lost, or damaged? We often tend to only understand the importance of something when it is no longer exists. Imagine that your company doesn't possess trust or professionalism and see how alarming it is.

Metaphysical resources influence performance directly and are particularly praised when an organization is in distress and all inner strength must be mobilized. Inner organizational strength comes not from buildings and machines, but from metaphysical resources which reside in people.

These resources have a strategic role for any organization. They are unique to every organization in the same way different combinations of people are unique. They cannot be precisely transferred or copied. Every organization has its own composition of metaphysical resources which defines it qualities and inner energy.

Imagine an equation in which $1+1=3$. This idea is highly prevalent in management circles. It seems that tangible resource plus intangible resource plus something mystical or invisible equals three, and everyone is satisfied with that explanation. What is the missing or invisible element that makes the equation work? That element is made up of metaphysical resources. Like a magical golden dust, metaphysical resources turn often irrational human emotions and inner feelings into the rational forces behind successful organizational performance.

Each metaphysical resource has its own importance for achieving the organization's goals. However, a single one can't cover all functions. They are best viewed as a package. Taken together, these metaphysical resources can supercharge an organization when properly utilized. Having an understanding of the nature and roles of metaphysical resources makes it possible to manage them and shape them into desired forms demanded by an organization's purpose and goals.

Power Pyramid

In the case of a hierarchy of symbols, values, rules, and attributes we look at them from top to bottom. When looking at the factors involved in generating and maintaining energy in an organization, we should look from the bottom to the top of this "power pyramid." We can envision a power pyramid which consists of four layers.

The first or bottom layer represents energy roots or factors influencing the input of every employee. This layer represents positive input, i.e. job satisfaction, respect, involvement, loyalty, shared affection, preparedness for change, and responsibility, as well as negative forces such as dishonesty, lack of authenticity, etc. If an amount of positive energy prevails over negative energy then it goes to the next level.

All energy from individual sources flows upward, forming metaphysical reservoirs or energy pools of different characteristics and purpose. The second layer represents metaphysical resources available to the organization.

The third layer represents the organization's actual performance level. Performance directly depends on the quality of the metaphysical resources generated in an organization.

The goal is placed on the pinnacle of the power pyramid. This is the fourth or the top layer of the power pyramid. Successful achievement of the organization's goal directly depends on a high level of performance and can't be realized without it.

The power pyramid is located inside of a sphere which represents an organization's vision. Vision defines goals and the type of metaphysical resources necessary to bring life to the vision. Vision and goals remain relatively constant, whereas the level of performance and quality of metaphysical resources are variable depending on the quality of the energy outputs from every organization's member.

Discussion

Metaphysical resources define the nature of psychological power residing in an organization's soul, or culture. Whether or not this potential is realized depends on how effectively it is exploited. Echoing Stephen R. Covey, "Ineffective people live day after day with unused potential" (Covey 2013, 276), we can say that inefficient organizations suffer every day having their potentials unused. The reason is simple. Organizations often neglect their most valuable asset, metaphysical resources. It is like sitting on a diamond mine while begging for change on the street. In practice, modern business can't afford such behavior.

Would you ignore love and care as mandatory features of happy family life? The more you put into the cultivation and nurturing of these feelings, the stronger and happier your family will be. The same happens with metaphysical resources which can be of a different quality. They can be very powerful and efficient, making culture positive and super productive if cared for. At the same time, metaphysical resources can have negative value and work against the organization, turning culture counterproductive.

Metaphysical resources are not given or acquired from external suppliers but grown from within an organization and demand positive thinking and masterful management.

Practical Tips

- Metaphysical resources don't tolerate a passive approach and erode fairly quickly.
- Make treating and caring for metaphysical resources a habit, in the same manner as a company protects its stock.
- Take care of metaphysical resources without compromising one for another. Doing so will place performance and achieving the organization's goals in jeopardy.
- Metaphysical resources don't demand expensive warehouses but they are always valuable and necessary for success.
- Metaphysical resources can be viewed as a secret weapon in the market. Be generous to your own people and don't let the competition in on the secret.
- The prospects for metaphysical resources development are limitless.
- Metaphysical resources are effective to the extent organizations recognize them. The more you see in them, the more effectively metaphysical resources work for an organization. Get the most out of them.
- Whether you believe in metaphysical resources, high performance can't be achieved without them.

- Compassionately focus on developing metaphysical resources and owners and employees will be always satisfied with the result of the organization's activity.

CHAPTER SIX

CHANGING, NOT BENDING

"Whosoever desires constant success must change his conduct with the times."

- Niccolò Machiavelli

What is Change?

A company is not a *Perpetuum Mobile,* running forever with no external input. It demands a constant supply of fuel, maintenance, and frequent fine-tuning of all its systems. Like individuals, a company must constantly strive for improvement to stay alive, and that requires hard work and willingness to change.

People frequently make use of leisure, silence, and contemplation to gain an understanding of themselves, and to decide what and how to change to become stronger individuals. Companies must also strive for this kind of self-awareness. The difference is that a company can't afford such moments of stillness. In today's extremely dynamic marketplace, organizations of many kinds experience pressure from both internal and external forces. Thus, it is vital to see a need for change in order to unlock hidden potential.

With all frequent environmental and market changes, managing how those changes affect the organization's culture is a vitally important task. Managing culture involves navigating an organization through the debris of environmental obstacles and storms to the promised land of long-term success.

Ultimately cultural change needs to be managed so that people's qualities and competences are coordinated to achieve the organization's vision. Change is by its nature difficult to predict. It is just as difficult to understand the consequences of our reactions to it. While changing one thing, a number of other factors need to be considered and all possible harmful side effects taken into account. Change, as you can see, requires the efforts of everyone affected by it.

Why Do We Need Change?

We don't plan our past, only the present and future. Drinking coffee, we charge ourselves with caffeine to help get through the immediate future. Negotiating a deal is about securing a profit in the future not in the past. Likewise, change is directed toward the future and not to the past.

Yes, if we forget about the past then we lose a foundation for shaping the future. If we can't change now, then the future is questionable. Whereas, each organizational generation is a cognitive link between the past and the future in a chain of organizational history, and thus defines the long-term strategy and demand for change in order to be prepared for the future. If the present generation of employees is not aware of the company's past and is not thinking about the future, then there is no chance for such a company to survive as this history chain will snap before long.

Disruption of commonness is a property of those who strive to create a bright tomorrow. However, it is not possible to create a bright future without fixing present problems and weaknesses, where impossible is the word for those not prepared to change. This word is right out of the Dark Kingdom dictionary. Witnessing daily changes around us and doing nothing, waiting for a catharsis to happen, equals a predictable hand-made catastrophe. Refusal to change is like conscious refusal of reality, resulting in a loss of control over the products.

Culture demands regular shaping because of environmental changes caused by variables in customer demands, competition, new technologies, and industry practices. The company's culture is getting stressed as it faces a sudden growth in the size and scale of it operations, aging, operational principle, and quality of available human resources.

Aiming to release the full potential of culture and its internal energy, managers can begin to feel like hamsters in a wheel – analyzing the present shape of culture, choosing the best way to improve, and implementing the necessary changes. It is not easy as one often finds dead ends, and must come back to the beginning starting the process all over again. Frustration with this is nothing new, growth means accepting change. The process is often painful, but as they say in the sports world, "No pain, no gain."

The manager must be alert for signals of forthcoming changes by listening to customers and observing even small events and accidents. Ignoring these clues can result in a once familiar environment changing into something strange and threatening.

Especially, while establishing a new business venture, one should be prepared to embark on a path of constant change. Too often, beginning entrepreneurs leave things to chance, expecting to catch a break to be able to then sit back and relax. Any serious and successful entrepreneur knows this is the furthest thing from reality.

Purpose of Change

When defining the purpose of change one should speak simply and clearly. Change is optimization of an organization's culture, adapting it to new situations. Not forcing people to change is what causes stress and blocks your employees' potential.

Change requires the wisdom to see things differently, not in a patterned or trendy way, while avoiding common mistakes. The ability to plan with an eye to the future and not staying stuck in the same ways of doing things is must for any competent manager.

Cultural change means growing people's qualities and allowing people to find ways to use them for the good of the company. An old Chinese proverb says: "If you want one year of prosperity, grow grain. If you want ten years of prosperity, grow trees. If you want one hundred years of prosperity, grow people."

Strategic or value-oriented change is focused on making a company stronger, allowing the company and its members to face the future without fear. To do this, managers have to focus on rewarding and developing their employees. Doing so will help them to become more professional and productive.

In terms of culture, we aim to make changes when the company becomes stagnate. Those changes aim to improve internal and external processes, scale up, or revitalize inner positive forces.

An organization must always be ready to change. In any process, weakness will be exposed as new circumstances are encountered. It is essential to have a basic plan to implement these revitalizing changes in place. These changes aim to:

- To discover potentials. No stone should be left unturned when evaluating what is going on inside an organization, and what employee potentials are not being tapped. Uncovering and stimulating that potential can help drive new innovations.

- To recognize gaps and inconsistencies. The purpose is to determine whether the state of culture is in good shape, needing only minor improvements or in need of complete overhaul.

- To ignite employees' willingness to change. Walk before you run. Implement minor but important changes and by doing so, get employees prepared for major changes. Let them feel the success of small changes before implementing big ones.

- To enhance the role of cultural values. The purpose is to revitalize the importance of values and align people around them. Don't let the importance of the company's values erode.

Changes for improvement can be addressed at every stage of development as a necessary part of organic growth:

- To enhance performance by enriching metaphysical resources. Metaphysical resources demand constant revitalization and enrichment through increased effort of employees. Otherwise, their value will decline and become corrosive.

- To improve the volume and quality of human energy sources. The aim of change is to repurpose non-effective energy sources and put them to work for the company. For instance, it was proved that enhanced loyalty increases productivity by eleven percent.

Scale-up changes needed:

- To prepare for the next stage of strategic development. Continuous growth assumes stages where some forces will become conflict. This demands occasional revision of rules and codes of conduct.

- To eradicate negative side effects of growth. For example, employees can become disconnected concentrating on processes rather than on people.

- To improve consumer attractiveness and social recognition. The bigger a company gets, the more stakeholders are involved in its processes and influenced by its activity.

This results in the organization becoming faceless and impersonal. Keeping itself attractive to people outside the organization through enhancement of inner qualities is a must.

- Leveraging the impact of technological advances. Implementation of new technologies often leads to the resetting of roles and organizational relationships, demanding a great deal of team training, mutual support, and coordination.

Principal changes are needed to eradicate major problems with culture or when organizations develop Dark Kingdom-like traits. When this occurs, a major top-to-bottom overhaul of the culture is required. That overhaul must address the following:

- Loss of cultural functions. When a culture is not functioning as desired, its values are vague and its efficiency plummets. This demands serious action and great care in order to resurrect the culture.

- Recovering the human nature of the organization. The purpose is to revise a role of symbols, values, and rules completely, along with stimulating positive input of every employee, revealing new positive potentials within the organization.

- Damaged or undeveloped organizational relationships (internal and external). People separated by a negative culture need to be reinvigorated in a positive environment.

- Delayered culture. We can often see that managers from upper hierarchical levels don't see what is going on at the other levels. These layers are often artificial and often prevent people from having a full view of a company's situation. This creates a kind of selective blindness which results in the formation of encapsulated groups that are at odds with one another and even with the company.

This is only a general guideline. A number of other suggestions can be added to this list depending on circumstances, present state of the culture, and organizational goals. In any case, the importance and necessity of change in any given situation should be gauged against corporate values and impact on the development of human qualities.

Planning Change

Any change begins with a vision. Vision is a visualization of a desired future and the determination of what needs to be done to make it a reality. Vision requires us to be prepared for serious changes. Preparing organizations for change means getting employees to ask questions and to see, think, and do differently.

Every serious change should be seen as a new stage, not just in the organization but in its employees as well.

A Canadian businessman once told me:

"I feel like a child every time I'm implementing change or starting new things again, from scratch, working to grow to an adult within a month or two."

See the new challenges as a child and consider the change completed when you and your employees have become confident in the new paradigm. Then be ready to do it all again. There are several stages to this complex journey:

- Have a clear vision of change and define its goals. Planning and implementing change requires employees' buy-in to a system of forward thinking. Without this buy-in, what should be a positive change can wind up bending and even breaking employees, adversely affecting the culture, and undermining your initial goals. Establishing buy-in starts from a clear definition of purpose and goals, so members of the organization understand why the changes are being implemented.

- When an organization's goals change, values may also need to be changed. This is critical to realizing what problems need addressing while understanding that the true problems are often hidden. This happens when managers take for granted that their employees understand the new goals and will simply adjust accordingly.

- See what you have at hand. Growing a tree needs fertile soil. A company's past is the best fertile soil or foundation for moving forward. Recall the lessons learned through past successes and failures in order to understand from where the company started. A solid knowledge of where you are at present and what you have at hand is crucial to get to where you want to go. Not doing so will lead to managers believing they have tools and processes at their disposal that simply aren't there. As Peter Drucker wrote in his article in the Wall Street Journal "Don't Change Corporate Culture: Use It!" "Company cultures are like country cultures. Never try to change one. Try, instead, to work with what you've got." (Drucker 1991, A14) Most resources needed for change are already within the company, and every employee is a resource carrier. Therefore, change is a matter of planning and thinking rather than budget. Once managers understand the present state of the company and clearly present their vision of its future, the employees will marshal their resources to implement it.

- Maintain a support base on all levels. It is difficult and time consuming to get every individual on board with change, particularly in large organizations. This is especially true across peer groups as it is human nature to have better cognitive understanding with peers than with those outside the peer group. Nominate change scouts who are going to lead change on every level and in every department. They will help communicate the new process to different peer groups through every stage of change.

- Get management strongly involved. If you want your employees to change, show them that you are changing as well. Employees will support the change to the same as extent as their leaders, thus it is important for company management to be actively involved with their sleeves rolled up. It has a three-in-one effect – employees see their managers taking the change seriously, they are quick to spot how their leaders are getting rid of their own bad habits and inefficient practices, and they will follow the new practices with greater speed and enthusiasm.

- Maintain control over change processes. Change processes demand control and alignment of every single step. Therefore, they must be checked and revised regularly, like checking on a patient in critical care. The role of change scouts is inevitable during transition times. Also, organizational change is an excellent way to recognize and eliminate recusant employees who do more harm than good to a firm. Let cultural homeostasis do its job.

- Be prepared for alignment. A long transition can be interrupted by environmental or market changes which can affect the original goals, and likely will require a revaluation and realignment of goals and the approach taken up till that point. Blindly ignoring these situations will bog the organization down in a swamp of process that is no longer viable.

- Avoid a clash of cultural and architectural codes. To enable the positive results of a revitalizing change to take effect, rules must be revised in accordance with the new vision of values and inner organizational goals. This often means a change of an organization's architectural codes. Architectural codes represent a system of directly enforced rules and practices which are usually written in various company documents. They are different in nature to cultural codes which represent a system of indirectly enforced rules. Cultural codes are usually tacit and residing in the minds of employees. Significant problems arise from the clash of cultural and architectural codes. They become a two-component explosive which can completely destroy an organization. Architectural changes can be viewed as cultural clash initiators. The reason is simple – rules are more malleable to the decision makers at all levels, who are not always acting for an organization's good, by manipulating rules at their personal discretion. Thus, rules should be adjusted to the cultural values and norms of an organization because they are the genetic codes that guide its development.

Enemies of Change

Human psychology resists change and removing employees' psychological barriers is an enormous task. Any change splits employees into supporters and non-supporters. Even Moses, who sought to lead people away from brutal slavery and into freedom, had doubters before and even after crossing the Red Sea. Often, people prefer the devil they know to the angel they don't.

It would be wonderful if changes in the workplace happened instantaneously with the champagne already chilled, waiting for celebration. However, change requires long-term commitment and the ability to overcome the enemies of change, natural fears and psychological inertia, which reside in any company.

Employees are often afraid of losing their job security as a result of changes in the company. This is understandable if the goals are not thoroughly and enthusiastically explained. Otherwise, they may think that a necessity for change means the organization is dying, with the change just delaying the inevitable. Change demands a clear and detailed explanation that it is a matter of reaching new heights and responding to changing circumstances in order to avoid the mentality of fear. Should that kind of negative thinking take hold, employees will become cynical and even more resistant to change?

Peter Drucker wrote in the article "Managing for Business Effectiveness" in Harvard Business Review, "What is the major problem? It is fundamentally the confusion between effectiveness and efficiency that stands between doing the right things and doing things right. There is surely nothing quite so useless as doing with great efficiency what should not be done at all" (Drucker 1963). People resist if they see change as meaningless or as some sort of exercise in management's ability to exert power. Such resistance can occur at all levels of personnel. Employees' confidence will grow if they see that the forthcoming change will be addressed in the context of the company's values and that it has a genuine purpose that will benefit the company and, along with it, its employees.

Uncertainty leads to increased stress levels and frantic queries. This issue is particularly transparent in countries with a high cultural index of uncertainty avoidance, such as Turkey, Greece, Russia, and Japan (Hofstede 1980). Employees need to see a plan that is well laid out, with clearly defined stages and realistically projected outcomes.

A lack of confidence is a natural response to questioning management's view of our personal competence. Will the company still value me with my dated skills and competences? I am too old or insufficiently trained? Will I feel lost?" The employee's depth of commitment to and involvement in job-related tasks, sense of personal satisfaction and self-respect may all be perceived to be under threat. Firm reassurance of their value for the company combined with appropriate training can diminish this unpleasant feeling.

Stability, patterned and predictable events, gives people a sense of controlling their own future, or being builders of their own destiny. A sense of frustration takes hold when their expectations are collapsed because of an unpredictable forthcoming change process. Without adequate preparation, employees may not be able to envision the results of change. Patterned thinking due to established routines and habits could limit enthusiasm for change, particularly for those employees who are fairly settled and may not be prepared to change things as simple as an everyday travel route or dress code. Only patience and persistence in making new things familiar to employees can help in such cases.

Who will remain energized and focused going through an endless cycle of transition after transition? Endless change leads to fatigue. The longer it goes, the more resistance it causes. In truth, not all change inevitably becomes successful, particularly those that are ill-conceived and poorly executed due to inadequate planning and preparation. Occasionally, with the goal of demonstrating that actions and changes are being implemented, management often irresponsibly jumps from one extreme to another. By respecting employees, management also protects them from such rash decisions.

People protect their familiar cultures and are prepared to fight for them to be protected and maintained. If a cultural violation is noticed, their resistance becomes stronger depending on the degree of violation. However, it can be difficult to recognize and articulate where such resistance originates, as the inner organization's opposition is not always prepared to step forward. This may divert attention to non-cultural matters shifting focus away from problem-solving actions.

Therefore, jumping the gun with sudden changes is more likely to cause resistance rather than generate support. Thus, warm up the culture to prepare it for change, skip issues which may be irrelevant or can be revisited later, focus on its effects on people, and be ethical in its implementation.

Change is a long transition process where internal relationships are at their most fragile and an organization's core components of trust, shared vision, and teamwork must be carefully maintained to mitigate their potential dissolution. Give people what they need most at such moments – explanations, support, mentoring, and appreciation of their effort. Respect people and people will respect you in a mutual recognition of challenges faced by all parties. Share your vision with employees who will be taking an active role in it, and gain supporters one-by-one.

Weeks or Months

Initiate motivated change now and you'll be rewarded in the future. Motivated change is where the future is a motivational factor itself. Real motivation goes beyond immediate gratification in the short term, an attribute of human nature in today's society, reinforced by our technological advances of the last twenty years. However, change is a sensitive and long-term process which doesn't tolerate rashness. The art of transition assumes a long cycle of purposefully eliminating excessive processes which demands time. Lao Tzu in his *Tao Te Ching* reminds us: "Nature does not hurry, yet everything is accomplished."

How long is required to complete a cultural change? No definite answer is possible due to the complexity of the combination of involved variables and the inability to accurately predict the outcome of change's implementation. Culture is not something than be created into being with a snap of the fingers.

The growth cycle of bamboo provides a useful illustration of the value of patience and perseverance. Moso is a temperate species of giant bamboo. It has edible shoots but is mainly used for textiles. Many of us have it in our clothing or linens. Besides its usefulness, moso bamboo is very peculiar timber species. It demands years of patience and daily work to grow. A small forty-centimeter sprout should be planted one meter deep in fertile soil, where it must be watered every day for five years. Miss one and the tree will die. You will see one shoot of moso on the 1825th day. A mere six weeks later, it will have grown to its average height of twenty-eight meters.

One can say that it took six weeks to grow; another will argue that it takes more than five years. While shaping culture, one needs to seed vision and trust in each employee to encourage belief in the organization and its goals. It must be watered and fertilized with effort, inspiration, and encouragement every day for a long time. People will give their hearts and minds to a cause if it can be made personal. In time, the entire organization will reap the fruits of mutual effort and patience.

How will we know when the change process has completed and the fruit is ripe? Change is completed when people stop talking about it, when the results of the change are now so incorporated into daily routine that they're taken for granted. A completed change is one that has moved from one of daily effort to a corporate success story of overcoming adversity and building a better organization for all.

The results of change can be seen in a number of factors such as what has been learned in the process, how the organization's culture has increased in strength and productivity, and in a rudimentary measure of what remains to be accomplished to achieve accomplishment of the organization's goals. It is important that all, top-management, line staff, external stakeholders, and customers be able to see and appreciate results of the change process.

Results of change can be viewed at a wider angle by asking what kind of footprint this change left on the lives of everyone involved? Would it be good, bad, or leave no footprint at all? These important questions are not to be forgotten while planning to shape any organization's culture.

Post-Change Adaptation

Change confirms the accomplishment of a particular stage of an organization's development. A new stage of development is inevitable in this fast changing world, an inevitability for which an organization must remain prepared. When such goals have been accomplished, however, there is a post-change stage that should be considered. The post-change period is a time to adapt to new qualities and roles.

In practice, few companies survey whether their employees believe in the organization's purpose and goals, and whether or not they are satisfied with company behavior after change. Often, things seem fine on the surface when, in actuality, they are not. A feeling of tension in relationships reflects hidden conflict of interests and perspectives. The issue is simple; some employees enthusiastically welcomed and embraced the change, while others just passively followed along. However, we all know that even dead fish follow the stream.

It is crucial to learn whether or not existing employees are feeling satisfied and rewarded by the changes once they have been implemented. Do they believe the promises meant to stimulate their efforts have been fulfilled or that the leaders simply manipulated them, cheating them of any anticipated benefits? Do employees feel satisfied with their own professional growth and financial compensation? If not, their belief in the organization's culture will be destroyed and any benefits gained from the changes will be short lived.

A growing organization demands the inflow of new talents and directly influences changes in hiring practices, reward and bonus structures, and training modalities. More successful companies are looking for stronger skill sets which demand greater financial commitment for the long-term benefit of the organization.

Discussion

Change must be thoughtful and purposeful. For instance, changing rules and presenting new meaningless attributes doesn't mean changing something for good. It may result in more resistance and cynicism than in actual acceptance. Also, change doesn't mean bending employees and ignoring their perceptions. Doing so will simply lead to the fragmentation of the organization.

Change means investing in people and developing their talents and skills, their metaphysical resources. Such investment always returns through higher performance and increased potential. Change is an investment in the present generation of employees for a better future for the whole organization. Strengthening culture, impacting employees' thinking and behavior, enhancing the role of values, and enriching metaphysical resources is a never-ending process of management duties with great strategic importance.

Practical Tips

- If we consider that change is a path to a future, then a necessity for learning new skills and competencies is inevitable. Therefore, collective and individual learning are beneficial for change. Be prepared to cover these costs.

- Learn to communicate about change effectively before implementing. Failure here allows employee fears to grow.

- Change is important if it fits into the company's strategy. Therefore, in order to gain support during transition, employees should be aware of the necessity of change in the realization of strategic goals.

- Mentors and change scouts are needed to help fellow employees shift mentalities and overcome frustration.

- Change gives management and employees the opportunity to learn a great deal about one another, revealing undeniable truths.

- Similar to fly-fishing, where one needs to change a fly if conditions change from bright sunshine to overcast, be prepared to amend change processes if the environment and conditions have altered since implementation.

- Metaphorically, change can become like a civil war, with the repercussions of dividing and destroying the organization if not managed carefully.

- Whatever the result of change, people should feel that their efforts are appreciated. This will increase employee satisfaction and make them less resistant toward further changes.

- Never listen to suggestions from people who are not willing to implement change within themselves.

- Demonstrate sincere appreciation to employees for going through the rough times of change in tangible forms of increased reward.

CHAPTER SEVEN

THE ART OF BEING
TRUE TO SELF

"Your strength is not directly linked to your outer formation, but only through the image that remains in you."

C. G. Jung

We hear a myriad of opinions and suggestions on how to get focused, be confident, and strengthen the inner self as a matter of wellness, quality living, and success. People are considered strong if their two cores, physical and psychological, are in harmony. Bone, muscle, and tissue form the human body, providing the ability to conduct all physical activities. We tend to focus on strengthening our physical capabilities; however psychological strength residing in both soul and mind makes us thinking, feeling, imagining, and believing beings. To become more intelligent, focused, and resistant to life's challenges, we must nurture both inner and outer strength.

Organizations, similar to humans, also have two cores, physical and psychological. Organizational physical strength is defined by the rationality of the organization's structure and the effectiveness of its processes and functions. However, an organization's muscles cannot move it far without that critical power which is hidden in an organization's inner strength – its culture. A strong organizational culture allows its employees to collectively move forward and to face challenges with conviction and determination. Authenticity, advanced decision-making, preparedness for change, and elasticity of organizational mind are also shaped and driven by organizational culture.

Positive personal qualities are assets for every human. They are genetically imprinted, nurtured, and developed in a course of a life, making each person unique. If we feel depressed, weak, anxious, or unfocused, we are encouraged to heal our soul, the psychological part of our being. We want to preserve our authenticity and improve ourselves to become better than before. The impact of others on our lives, changes in living conditions, and circumstances of life are all influential in making one stronger or weaker depending on how strong one's soul and mind are.

In an organizational context, cultural qualities form an invaluable asset. Like every other asset, culture demands regular evaluation and nourishment to maintain its fullest value. Culture is unique for every organization and cannot be replicated, which makes it an indispensable advantage in competition. However, the dynamic nature of organizational life, due to changes in management and the never-ending influence of external forces, has an inevitable impact on organizational culture. Culture, despite the qualities imprinted at the company's founding, remains an asset and demands regular checkups. If changes result in positive enhancements, evaluation is still necessary in order to comprehend positive lessons learned as tools for the future. It is just as important for an organization to recall its positive achievements as its negative.

Show Your ID

How can organizational culture be described without using formalized definitions and academic jargon? Culture is the name for an organization's inner world, which consists of human feelings and attitudes towards colleagues and the organization itself. The inner world defines the pattern of interaction, trust, and cooperation forming an organizational identity. The twenty-first century demands a corporate identity that reflects the emphasized role of a company's employees and how an organization portrays itself to all external stakeholders. Identity expresses values, beliefs, and the professional traits of employees, which become visible to insiders and outsiders through an organization's culture. This is a manifestation of how employees see themselves and how others see them from the outside.

Identity is how members see and feel themselves being part of the organization and so affects how they behave among colleagues and toward the organization. "I am a supply manager" or "I am a supply manager and I work for company X". Can you see the difference in responses from people working for different companies in terms of culture? The first one is more likely to be working for a company with deflated culture, not rushing to be identified with that company. The positive reaction of the second respondent seems to indicate an individual who is a proud part of a particular organization, which spreads even further to influence the initial impression we form of the organization.

There is no secret that honest and transparent self-awareness and self-evaluation is a point of departure in soul healing. The same can be suggested to organizations that care about strengthening their life-giving asset, culture.

One may ask what the difference is between image and reputation. Image is an impression external stakeholders have about an organization, where reputation is grounded in actual experience.

The difference can be explained in a simple way - a wolf in a sheep's skin, where the wolf is the actual identity, and the sheep's skin is a cloak to mask the wolf's true identity. Thus, you have the image of a sheep and reputation of a nasty predator.

Identity is a by-product of image and reputation. By looking at an organization's identity, we can estimate its cultural portrait. Such a portrait is more real than a financial statement which can be edited or purported reviews from happy customers being written by company staff. Identity is formed in the minds of an organization's members, mirroring the cultural qualities of the organization. It cannot be faked. Show me your company's cultural ID and I will predict your company's future.

Who Am I - Introvert or Extrovert?

We tend to judge someone's personality as falling into one of two categories - introverts or extroverts. This method of identification can tell us a lot about one's personality and manner of interacting with the world. Introverts are self-energizing and mentally look inwards. The word introvert comes from the Latin *intro-vertere* meaning to turn inward. Extroverts are completely opposite, deriving energy from others, actively interacting with the external world with an outward focus. It is difficult to find someone who is purely introvert or extrovert, as people are often a bit of both and may demonstrate different behaviors depending on circumstances.

Extroverts are energized by socializing and group activity, which enhances their creative processes, whereas quieter environments allow introverts to achieve the focus necessary for them to perform at the best of their abilities. It seems that people from different archetypes have different compositions of neurons in their cerebral cortex that make them more comfortable and successful in different environments and in performing different types of mental activities. No one can escape his or her inborn temperament, but we can learn to how it benefits us or how it can also serve to hinder us. Even a very young child shows this inborn temperament by the manner in which they approach new people or situations, by either marching right in or by holding back and evaluating.

Do organizations differ from humans in psychological terms? Similar to humans, organizations can be considered as introverts or extroverts depending on the organizational archetype, i.e. the core resources used in its processes. The cultural type is the actual organizational identity which remains with it forever. Being an introvert or extrovert is neither exclusively good nor bad for an organization. This is a quality that allows company culture to shine in a certain light. The properties of the relevant cultural type allow an organization to reveal its inner capacities in terms of the generation of value.

The mode of cultural type defines the relative autonomy of organizational behavior, development of organizational capabilities, relationship development, and psychological patterns of decision-making. All of these allow the organizational mind to remain focused on the effective execution of goals and keeping members enthusiastically engaged.

According to Scott Barry Kaufman, "the more people were acting extroverted and conscientious, the more they reported being in a positive mood and feeling lower levels of fatigue in the moment, but after three hours they reported higher levels of fatigue. The level of fatigue depended on the number of people met during the last hour, the intensity of the social interactions, and how much they had a specific goal in mind when they were studying or working. Interestingly, these effects were found for both introverts and extraverts. Nevertheless, there are real differences between introverts and extroverts that shouldn't be ignored. For one, introverts really do prefer solitude and quiet time more, on average, than extroverts. Also, the latest science of introversion suggests that extroverts are more driven to engage in social interactions that particularly increase social status or social attention. Extroversion seems to be fueled by dopamine, particularly through the reward circuits of the brain that cause us to get excited by the possibility of 'appetitive rewards' in the environment, such as money, power, sex, and social status." (Kaufman 2016).

Introverts and extroverts show different behavior in the process of achieving goals. The biggest difference between introverts and extroverts in an organizational context lies in goals, approaches in development of organizational capabilities, imprinted roles and functions, types of human capital, and thus behavior. Here we can draw a line between organization-introverts and organization-extroverts using archetypes offered by *Organisational Anatomy* – producers, knowledge-dependent, location-dependent, donor-dependent, and state-affiliated organizations (Konovalov 2016, 27).

There are two archetypes of organizations that can be considered as extroverts – location-dependent organizations such as hotels, supermarkets, shops, airlines, etc. and donor-dependent organizations such as charities and faith-based organizations. For such organizations and charities, maintaining recognition as an active part of a community's culture is critical in terms of financial support.

Producers and knowledge-dependent organizations, such as banks, universities, and hospitals are organization-introverts, which concentrate on precision of production by offering a quality product which serves to meet a community's need, and thus does not have the same level of need to be actively engaged in outreach to seek consumers. Their key to success is to provide services using the most current knowledge and technological advances available in their fields.

A state-affiliated organization can be introvert or extrovert depending on its role, whether it is security, defense, social service, and foreign or internal affairs. Social and administrative services are extroverts since they deal with the public. Authorities and state-affiliated bodies holding certain highly-classified secrets and protocols can be considered as introverts due to their explicit typology.

The nature of cultural type can also be correlated within an industry context. Industrial or professional context differs in terms of specific signals, codes, unspoken rules of engagement, communication styles, and perceptions of insiders and outsiders. High-context professions such as medical consultants, researchers, engineers, or architects, for example, use specific language and communication codes which clearly distinguish industry insiders from outsiders. They are introverts who are looking inside of their domains' boundaries and working in implicit environments. Their conversations are loaded with professional jargon which is unclear and almost mysterious to those from outside of their professions. Professional rapport is a prerequisite of successful dealing with these companies. It confirms that producers and knowledge-dependent organizations are introverts.

Extroverts represent low-context industries such as retail, charities, local utility supply, transport, etc., whose language and communication styles must be understandable for all. Access barriers and perceptions for outsiders are low so long as processes are explicit for all.

Similar to humans who can be a bit of both at different times, all organizations are in a position to express themselves differently from time to time. For instance, universities must run active recruitment campaigns, and producers cannot live without shouting about their latest product.

Identity, Once and Forever

An organization's purpose and its particular archetype is something cultural identity should consistently maintain for the life of the company. These are the stable features of an organization. Operational principles, whether being generalist or specialist, are chosen initially at the moment of business model development. It tends to remain a permanent characteristic. We can say that generalists are more likely to be extroverts as they tend to go after low-hanging fruit and must be at the center of public attention, whereas specialists are more likely to be introverts as they concentrate on quality, custom orders, and satisfying the demands of narrow groups of customers. Identity is genetically imprinted.

The only issues which tend to change are age and possibly size. The aging of an organization is associated with growth, i.e. change of size. On one hand, growth always demands an expansion of organizational boundaries. This demands enhanced public visibility, sophisticated exploitation of existing markets, penetration into new markets and active interaction with all groups of old and new stakeholders. Growth is the expansion of organizational networks and territories and consistently attracting new customers that replace those who leave. Without growth, there is a slow death of the organization.

On the other hand, growth demands bigger teams of employees working cohesively. Unfortunately, such expansions do not always run smoothly and it takes time before they become effective. This is like bringing a new member into a family. With a sudden growth of the family, less attention is paid to each individual member.

The tough realities of adopting new members into the organization and challenges from increased external interaction can lead to clashes during growth periods. A tension remains in place even after a period of expansion, before the process reaches a new equilibrium. If the growth is organically gradual, then all functions are growing evenly, adapting to the new realities. However, rapid growth has the side effect of weakening the organizational immune system. Leaders and managers can lose focus on the main goals as a result of having too much on their plates, new tasks and routines, and management of new entities. A growing number of employees add more challenges and problems. Veterans take the existing culture for granted and have difficulty explaining it and commonly accepted rules of interaction are widely broadcast within the organization. Newcomers are introduced to processes and seldom have a cultural guide around the company. New recruits also bring their knowledge of organizational culture from previous jobs. These different cultures – the previous company and the new – are not always compatible. Most likely, they have a different understanding of loyalty, commitment, and tolerance, and thus, affect a culture that is already stressed. Given these factors, expansion can be a threatening period for any organizational culture.

Discussing change in a company's culture, Peter Drucker (Drucker 1991, A14) suggested "it is best to work with what you've got." Preserving an organization's identity as its most valuable asset is critical for all organizations. Whatever is happening outside of the organization, the best thing is to remain true to self which will in turn keep the organization strong. Cultural type characterizes the way the company achieves its goals and mirrors its inner qualities. Adaptation of inappropriate cultural types inevitably leads to the internal conflict and potential loss of the company's competitive uniqueness, which is risky for performance and sustainability. In medical terms, depending on its severity, such organizational behavior can be diagnosed as depersonalization or even schizophrenia if it becomes sufficiently degraded.

Identity Is a Must

Famous psychologist Carl Jung, when discussing psychological archetypes in his letter to Eugen Bohler in December 1955, wrote, "In the first place it is they that do things with us and it is only afterwards that we learn what we can do with them." (Jung 1973, 56) Thus, full understanding of the relevant cultural type (ID) is a good way to recognize the full potentials of a company. Intelligent managers know how to organize processes, wise managers know how to unleash cultural strength by using advantages particular to the type of culture. For an organization, being true to itself is pragmatically rational. It allows:

- Increased value of intangible assets and mobilization of hidden capabilities, which has a direct positive impact on capitalization,

- Enhanced exploitation of human resources, nurturing employees' talents and qualities and thus increasing human capital,
- Enhanced ability to maintain effective external relations allows more efficient access to resources and increased social capital,
- Improved functions due to enhanced internal support, better communication and stimulating inner environment overall, all of which increase manageability,
- Attractiveness for external stakeholders – customers, suppliers, investors, creditors,
- Strong and clear image allowing focus on its own qualities and advantages,
- Avoidance of fatigue from cultural ambiguity,
- Endurance regarding environmental changes so no energy and resources are wasted.

Nineteenth-century American philosopher, William James, in his lecture before the Harvard Natural History Society, suggested that "the greatest discovery of my generation is that human beings, by changing the inner attitudes of their minds, can change the outer aspects of their lives." (James 1880) This is very true, but be careful as it works in both perspectives, positive and negative, depending on perception. Problems arise when a company causes ambiguity by using the wrong cultural ID and works towards goals which are inappropriate for the organizational archetype. By using a false or inappropriate identity, the organization shows an unnatural or artificial personality, which is unattractive and lacks integrity. Artificial personality leads to a loss of the archetype's advantages. Such an organization is diminishing the value of naturally given superior cultural qualities imprinted from the outset. For instance, it is never productive for hospital staff (organization-introvert) to expend too much of their precious time and energy on unnecessary external events, or for priests (organization-extrovert) to avoid talking with people and losing parishioners.

Companies can recognize their faults through fair evaluation or by looking at a rival's misconduct as something of a mirror. Carl Jung in *Memories, Dreams, Reflections,* suggested "everything that irritates us about others can lead to an understanding of ourselves." (Jung 1989, 208) If an organization misbehaves in accordance with the imprinted cultural type, then it should be ready for a number of setbacks which can dramatically affect organizational performance and damage the positive attitude of people working in the organization. It is noticeably incongruent when a company-introvert behaves as an extrovert, or a company-extrovert hides its talents. There are several critical problems in cases of identity conflict – withhold or splurge emotions, foggy identity, necessity for excessive control, professional mismatch, and marketability of the organization.

There is little chance to develop a strategic vision for leaders or employees if the company has an unclear identity. Vision and execution of strategic plans are correlated with enthusiasm, personal commitment, and effectiveness of teams. If people cannot see where they are going, then their commitment and enthusiasm will be severely lacking. While working for such a company, people consider their job as some sort of punishment, and are thinking of their own survival and not about team performance. Culture turns into an inhibitor.

Identity ambiguity reflects a deviation of the organization from archetype and market requirements. Let's imagine a bank which spends more funds on social events rather than on research and development (R&D), knowledge generation, and staff training. This bank leads itself to a dead end of losing core assets and knowledge, which cannot be compensated for by an elevated social status. Unique knowledge of managing money will secure profit, attractiveness for clients and positive recognition for being professional, which will naturally lead to wide public recognition and desired social status.

If an organization has doubts about its own identity, then imagine how doubtful the inner environment and behavior of its members will be. Wrongly formulated cultural values and beliefs mislead employees and diminish the value of talents. An unfriendly environment and low level of trust among team members is like a roller coaster for human emotions. Results become a secondary issue for people who hold their breath each morning, diving into an uncooperative pool of unfair internal competition and counterproductive formalities.

Control is the process of establishing and maintaining authority over the organization. A necessity for control is defined by the behavioral nature of inconsistencies and the underperformance of people, which remain the core focus of organizational control. Prominent organizational identity stimulates employees' commitment and trust, thereby reducing the need for excessive and costly control. Unclear identity causes emotional exhaustion which leads to an inevitable increase in the number of mistakes. Self-doubts also grow, resulting in increased governance costs and ineffectiveness of processes.

Professional mismatch is an extremely serious issue for all organizations. While seeking employment, people imagine using their talents to receive rewards and promotions based on their assigned position and duties within the company. But a perfect match is not always available due to a number of different factors. The professional mismatch causes doubts in employees' minds, as they cannot see an alignment of their talents with the organization's needs and goals, which causes the wasting of professional qualities. Members, new and old, concentrate not on priority tasks but on battling with formalities and internal intrigues. A culturally intelligent person will always choose an organization which is compatible with his personality and will leave an incompatible organization at the first opportunity, removing his knowledge and skills from the company. In this sense, an organization with counterproductive culture will face a situation where the quality of its workforce becomes far from desirable in a very short time. Also, we all know that unsatisfied people are only working for a paycheck; their creativity is blocked.

Simple and Reliable

Managers are in a race to keep their companies aligned with market trends and tendencies but often fall into a trap of following market gossips. Tracking each nuance of the market can increase organizational complexity and create dysfunction by adding unimportant peripheral functions, causing the organization to lose sight of its core mission. Do not doubt the wisdom of the free market invisible hand; it is perfect in culling dysfunctional companies out of the market and promoting companies with a coherent identity and strong culture. The market environment is always more clever than a single organization. There is no point in bending the backbone of a company, its cognitive structures, core values, and beliefs, for something very minor or illusive.

Strong culture allows the channeling of views, practices, and routines into effective and simple systems. In this sense, culture steps forward and makes the organization more focused and simple in terms of management. These inner effective systems allow development of focused strategies which demands less effort to implement and are advantageous in nature. However, it is a property of mature organizations that remain undeveloped in young companies.

In this sense, it is worth mentioning the additional role of ideology as a tool for effective merging of businesses-introverts and businesses-extroverts into one simple, strong identity. ID is a unity of like-minded people with similar traits.

Psychologically, we prefer to recognize a simple identity, whereas a complex identity is viewed as unreliable and risky. Would you deal with a stranger with a muddy identity? Customers are the same, preferring to deal with an organization with a prominent and simple identity.

Practical Tips
- ID remains constant even if the values have changed.

- Brand and ID are different things, similar to the difference between image and reputation.
- Inappropriate ID reduces brand value.
- ID is linked to the company mission through understanding of itself and ability to present the company to the external world.
- ID is particularly important for organizations acting internationally. Stepping into new territories as an unknown, makes it critical to demonstrate company nature to local customers.
- Overcomplicating is an enemy of cultural identity.

CHAPTER EIGHT

IDEOLOGY

"Neither a person nor a nation can exist without some higher idea."

- F. Dostoevsky

Ideology, a Matter of Scale

Ideology is often considered as being the same as culture or something similar to it, which is inaccurate. Culture defines effective norms of organizational members' interaction directed toward the achievement of organizational goals. Ideology is a completely different dimension of organizational existence. Ideology is a psychological goal itself. Ideology can be considered a long-term psychological and cultural strategy. In an organizational context, ideology is a set of long-term cultural and ethical ideas and ideals which provide a vision for the achievement of strategic goals. These goals should be acceptable and supported by all corporate citizens despite their roles, national identities, and internal subordination. Uniting different cultures together in this way will make them more productive and help establish undisputable control over an organization. Ideology provides individuals with a sense of unity with an organization or state, of common mission, and of being part of something bigger than themselves. In other words, pieces of bright ceramic should form a beautiful mosaic and not a mess of colors.

The bigger the body, the more difficult it is to manage, whether it is a state, army, or huge business. The economic and political power of large corporations often goes beyond the scale of some small countries. For example, the United States Department of Defense employs 3.2 million people which is equal to the population of Kuwait; Walmart with 2.1 million employees equals the population of Slovenia; the National Health Service (UK) can be matched with Gabon's population of 1.7 million people; G4S (UK) and Tata Group (India) employ more than 600,000 people each, which is equal to the population of Montenegro. So, any large organization can be viewed as a microstate. Thus, large corporations demand something great which helps them keep geographically separated units together.

Any large corporation is not merely an individual body, but more like a pack of living organisms which needs something to keep its individual units together, preserving their nature while directing this huge pack towards the same goals. Large multinational companies with different goals, complicated hierarchies, and thousands of employees need a system of ideals or ideas which give a sense of belonging to something big. The commonly used term, corporate citizen, underlines the scale of such organizations, which may consist of a number of business units with their own, and often different, cultural norms.

It is difficult or almost impossible to grow a large organization (or state) without losing cultural cohesion. Thus, some kind of a core must be inserted into it which holds all cultural factors, differences, and similarities together. It functions as a culture moderator, coordinating disparate business units, defining strategic development of a large organization. The answer to this problem is ideology.

Initially, the term ideology came from the French *idéologie* (from *idéo-* + *-logie*) in 1796, offered by Antoine Destutt de Tracy, as the science of how ideas take root. Very quickly, the term ideology was equated with philosophical doctrine and became a versatile political weapon actively exploited by Napoléon Bonaparte in order to abuse his political opponents.

The stronger the ideology, the stronger the corporation is. By using an example from the global context, we can infer the strongest global influencers are the USA or China, countries with traditionally strong ideologies. At the same time, countries with unformulated ideologies hardly get on the list, particularly newly formed states which are only developing their ideological vision.

Corporate ideology is almost the same as national ideology with some differences underpinning the role of corporations as huge production or service organizations. On one hand, ideology represents a set of members' beliefs with similar patterns of understanding of cause-and-effect relations; on the other hand it regulates managers' behavior. Ideology is a coherent set of beliefs and assumed roles commonly accepted by an organization's citizens.

Ideology defines the crucial spirit of the corporation and can help make it both wise and powerful. An ideology that leads to thinking many years or even generations ahead will give an organization an advantage over competition that thinks in the short term. Being a superpower is less a matter of resources, location, or aggressiveness than it is having a strong ideology that can motivate its people.

Let's think about ideology from a different perspective. Alexander the Great started his empire with a small army, great desire, and strong ideology. The Roman Empire was built around the *Pax Romana* which was unbreakable as long as culture and ideology remained strong. However, the Roman Empire disappeared with the weakening of its core ideological principles which were replaced by the dictators' ambitions and power.

Today, there are thirty-four newly formed independent countries that have appeared on the world map since 1990, such as former USSR republics, former Yugoslavia entities, Namibia, Czech Republic, and so on. However, none of them are rocketing into a top global position despite their natural and human resources and obvious market and production potentials. They are thinking about the growth of their GDPs, power distribution, infrastructure development, creation of new laws and regulations, and attraction of foreign investments from any possible source. The struggle for them is to get all their strength together using whatever resources are available and take a leap from there. They have resources but no cohesive vision to direct their use. Instead of increasing strength, they are often stuck in the same paradigm as previous generations. The problem is that none of them took care to develop and proclaim a clear ideology aimed at concentrating all internal capacities and forming a single vision for the decades ahead. Ideology should come first, organizing the disorganized in the name of a bright and secure future for all national or corporate citizens.

Many Cultures, One Ideology

No company can gain a competitive advantage without a strong organizational culture. No corporation can gain this unique advantage without powerful ideology embedded in its identity and strategy of development. Ideology leverages cultural differences, core capabilities, and discrepancies and variations in understanding of values among an organization's citizens. Thus, it provides a competitive advantage for a corporation united with commonly understood perception.

Social norms and social codes are different and very local even in neighboring territories or countries. They are unique in terms of culture, values, symbols, and the way business is conducted. The sociocultural environment of a branch in Australia would be very different from that of one in Denmark or Brazil. Local political forces and the current stage of economic development are also strong influences on all corporate business.

The world is made up of many differences. The business and cultural context in London is different from Manchester; New York will be different from Seattle; and, of course, Tokyo is much different from Barcelona. Norwegians stop work at 3:00 p.m. during summer months and there is very little chance of getting them to answer business calls after working hours; they have a casual dress code unless they are working in a bank or the head office of a large company, and prefer responding to important or even urgent emails at the end of the day. The Japanese work tirelessly, fulfilling every point in the operations manual and are fully devoted to corporate values with all their minds and hearts. The Mediterranean people are very relaxed and never miss taking a siesta. Being big and global places a tremendous importance on the role of ideology in bringing people with very different beliefs and values from different corners of the world together; and imprinting a single idea of a loyal corporate citizenship on all of them. A big corporation which acts globally, like the U.S. pharmaceutical giant Merck & Co., Inc., with 68,000 employees, has more than seventy branches worldwide, from the USA to Thailand, and all of them have different cultures, working values, and traditions which cannot be successfully managed without strong ideology.

On the other hand, a large company can act in one country, such as the British cancer research charity Cancer Research UK, funding over 4000 researchers and having over 40,000 volunteers. CRUK is established in different locations such as London, Belfast, Cardiff, and Birmingham. At the same time, this socially important charity must keep all these heroes fighting cancer working together as one powerful force. In one place, volunteers who collect donations need to be clear, straight to the point with a bit of informal chat; in another place, a successful approach demands focused pitch, delicate talks, and detailed professional explanation.

In their own terms, political parties can be considered as corporations too, politically-focused, donor-dependent large organizations with huge budgets and millions of members from different classes, backgrounds, and social roles. However, an individual's willingness to enter into relationships with a political party comes from acceptance of its key ideological points.

Logic of Ideology

The twenty-first century is a time to rethink the role of ideology. This is not only a matter of corporate survival, but also development of all humanity, on all levels, from corporate to state. Ideology plays the role of a moderator responsible for the development of harmonic relationships between an organization (state) and its members (citizens). Ideology is an agreement between people and an organization.

However, we can see examples where people are not rebelling against a state, but the state acting against its own people. An organization acting against its own members is inevitably doomed. No ideology means no actual agreement exists and only silent but dangerous confrontation is there.

Ideological development is not a simple task; it is more of a sophisticated science which demands exceptional strategic vision, cultural sensitivity, superior knowledge of internal and external processes, and political sensitivity. Three main roles of ideology in terms of its viability and positive effect on corporate performance must be considered - progressive decision-making, social responsibility, and preserving its dynamic nature (Goll and Sambharaya 1995, 824).

One of the dominant and most obvious roles of ideology is to establish a foundational doctrine of beliefs and ideas common for all corporate citizens. The ideology must also be sympathetic and viable to the numerous external stakeholders who accept and support the corporate activities. If people do not consider the ideology as socially significant and relevant to their beliefs, they tend to resist it. Ideology is part of the identity of any large organization or nation. This tremendously valuable and intangible asset defines corporate capabilities and growth potentials. At the same time, ideology is responsible for giving a sense of belonging to corporate citizens. People want to feel that they are a part of something really big (a corporation) and at the same time, feel like respected members of a small community of like-minded people (a local office). Ideology serves this faith-in-corporate function as well.

The logic of ideological development is based on the ability to unite and empower very different parts of a corporation, strengthening social and operational relations between all branches and units, keeping them focused on strategic goals and maintaining effective control over the corporation as a whole. This can be achieved by offering an effective set of cultural and social ideas based on identifiable experience. They link the interests of owners, leaders, and members and their values and conscious choices of collaboration. The exceptionally difficult task of corporate ideologists is to bring all those separate locally-imprinted ideas, values, and habits over to one condensed and powerful idea and make it effective for the foreseeable future.

Operating in different cultures can present challenges even when seemingly using the same language and terminology. This is because often the same words mean different things to people in different cultures. For instance, the common term democracy is considered differently by Americans, Chinese, Russians, or Greeks. This difference has a direct impact on how people view power hierarchy, formality, the way unethical decisions are tolerated, and how employees from different countries consider management's activities. Such misunderstandings can lead to large conflicts.

However, being a goal in itself, ideology plays a critical role in establishing authority and full control over an organization and in justifying the superiority of that authority. Thus, ideology has an instrumental role in strengthening hierarchical relations. We cannot imagine a successful situation where a squadron takes control of an army and defines its strategy. In another instance, if a body controls the soul, and not vice versa, the consequences are surely dramatic for such an individual. In this sense, ideology is planned and directed by upper management as the rule makers.

Inevitably, ideology shapes how corporate citizens think, talk, behave, execute their duties, solve problems, make decisions, and see the world. Every large corporation represents a population of separated organizations and business units, and thus can be considered as a social form with the same properties in terms of belonging, identity, reporting, and ownership. Therefore, a corporation must develop its own language for defining roles and descriptions of them. These roles must be clearly understandable by all corporate citizens. At the same time, ideology forms the same pattern of thinking, logic of reasoning, and decision-making.

Let's consider a pack of wolves where the most mature and strongest lead a hunt in which the youngest and weakest cover gaps in the chase and control the prey from the sides. They are different in strength and experience, but they are very effective together. Almost the same happens in corporations where branches have different roles, functions, and operational capacities. All parts are not equal but all are essential. Another role of ideology is to link and maintain consistent operational efficiency and synergy of functions across the entire body of a large organization.

People are much better at reaching goals when they are not looking at each other and competing but instead are looking forward together in the same direction toward the corporation's goals. They are efficient to the extent their relationships are efficient. Strength of internal and external relations defines the distance to resources, level of transaction costs, knowledge sharing effectiveness, and social unity of an organization. Therefore, a corporation is as efficient as the strength of its internal and external relations. Being a tremendous constructive power, ideology stimulates the maintenance of productive organizational ties and effective interaction.

Large organizations attract the interest of the general public and, thus, the media, whether they are making changes in top management, launching a new product, a scandal over faulty service, and the extent of transparency of reporting. In this sense, all issues are benchmarked against declared ideology and corporate social responsibility statements. Ideology can be viewed as the declared standard of corporate behavior and all good or bad issues are measured against it.

Corporations can count on a long-term existence when a strong ideology is responsible for the corporation's ability to learn and adapt to a changing market. Culture and ideology have superior roles in educating the hearts of members of a small company or of citizens of a large corporation. Severe competition and environmental forces demand enhanced organizational endurance and organizational cognition as a matter of survival, which cannot be developed without ideology playing a prominent role.

Ideology is a soft power which undisputedly influences corporate citizens and has a strong influence on others outside of a corporation. Being the psychological and cultural core of a large organization, ideology unites separated units into one, global-scale, unstoppable stream of power and productive expertise. Remove this core from the organization and it will fall to pieces, very soon becoming disorganized and an easy target for competitors.

The growth of an organization is accompanied with a growing number of shareholders or stockholders whose greatest concerns are performance and increased profit margins. They tend to forget that strong culture and ideology allowed that growth which initially attracted them. In their view, they are buying profit and not culture, and since profit has grown there is no point in spending too much time on culture. Leaders are responsible for this extremely important task of protecting the ideology and culture of their organizations from such unfriendly interventions.

CHAPTER NINE

LEADERSHIP: ORCHESTRATING VALUES

A vision and culture are born together in a leader's mind. As such, they can't exist independently of each other. While developing a wide vision encompassing a unique product, competitive market position, and satisfied customers, a leader is simultaneously envisioning the understanding of culture. The leader is defining roles, duties, the nature of relations, and the human qualities and values necessary for making the vision a reality. This makes leaders the primary persons responsible for the culture of their organizations.

The leader's vision defines the organization's symbols which express the necessary culture and the standards of behavior that will build and reinforce it.

There is some separation between vision and culture. Vision remains the domain of the leader whereas culture becomes the collective property of all members of the organization. Leaders must therefore take care of the culture. If they do not, it will become managed by "shadow" influencers, who will push it in a destructive direction. Still, the leader is responsible for it in much the same way as a parent is for one's own child. In the event the culture degrades, it is the leader's responsibility to recognize the demise and initiate action to repair the damage.

Orchestrating Values and Metaphysical Resources

Consider a conductor's movements during a performance. It looks as if he is spelling a magician's abracadabra, flapping his wand and the melody flows, touching the hearts of hundreds and thousands of listeners, setting their souls flying at that moment. Phenomenal conductors such as Herbert von Karajan and Sir Simon Rattle come to mind. Their work leaves no doubts why two words, conductor and leader, are synonyms. However, the conductor's real work begins behind the scenes as he works to guide the members of the orchestra into one synchronized body. In the hands of want-to-be leaders, the conductor's baton would produce a melody that would be horrible to the ears, and the conductor would be booed by the audience.

The same happens in the corporate world. A well-orchestrated culture inspires employees and customers alike. The achievement of each specific goal demands a certain configuration of the metaphysical resources. The leader must be able to intuit the values and psychological state of the employees and use sophisticated knowledge to draw out their talents in the service of the larger vision. Knowing one's immediate subordinates in such a way will allow the leader to arrange them in such a way in the organization that their talents and qualities reinforce each other, leading to the group's best possible performance.

Every corporate success story involves a unique composition of resources, including metaphysical resources and the leadership qualities and corporate culture that made it possible. By finding the optimum configuration of values and metaphysical resources, a leader is able to unleash the hidden power in an organization. A leader must be skillful in managing culture, in order to prevent it from transforming from a beautiful melody to a miserable cacophony. Clearly, such a negative spiral will destroy the organization from the inside.

Being at the top of the organization gives the leader a panoramic view. It also carries great responsibility.

A Scottish acquaintance related this story:

"The best leadership lessons I learned, I learned from my first skipper, Jack, at the age of twenty-three. I knew that it was a tough job for tough guys but decided to try. Jack

was famous for good catches, the best crew, and calmness. He called me in as soon as I stepped on board and asked why I decided to go to sea and what I was aiming to earn. When I told him my desired figure, he thought for a moment and said, "You will get more if you work hard, help others on deck, and understand that all of us are getting shares which come from a joint effort. Help others and they will help you." I made more than expected on that trip and all other trips with Jack. I learned my first valuable lessons on how to be a leader by motivating people, getting them together, respecting aims and desires, and being supportive of people. The best memories are of how we worked together like a Swiss-made watch, as champions, and not about storms and bloody blisters. Today, being a GM in the fishing industry, I always recall Jack's lessons when it comes to issues of maintaining a strong company – be part of a team, learn as much as you can about your people, gain as much as possible for the team and thus, for yourself, and get back home safe."

Use every opportunity to strengthen culture and enhance metaphysical resources. There is always a chance to advance values and provide chances to employees to exercise their qualities and thus, to enhance metaphysical resources. It consists of treating employees with respect, talking with people about where the company is going, listening to their initiatives and suggestions, and simply keeping contact with the team. Making duties meaningful is vitally important and highly motivational in itself. A few words of appreciation and support can drive employees' motivation for a long time. Talk with people and let them respond. It gives employees a feeling of security and control, and allows one to feel as if they have a sense of what is happening in the organization.

An organization, like bamboo, needs daily watering but, as a result, can result in enormous growth. It will reward your effort by becoming productive and responsive to the organization's needs.

Successful change is managed by leaders who inspire their people by injecting them with confidence while facing tough challenges and uncertain events, by being a model of perseverance and open-mindedness. Good leaders build better futures. A boardroom is like a control panel which receives signals from both internal systems and the external environment. If the board is correctly analyzing this input, changes will be made for the organization's benefit. Changes made from the bottom, often with incomplete information, will often lead to chaos. Thus, change is most successfully implemented by leaders who see the need and are ready for change. Successful change demands the leaders to be a model for their employees.

Advancing the qualities of others by mentoring, training, and supervising them is a duty and privilege of the responsible leader. Leadership is all about growing qualities and revealing talents to build the value of both employees as individuals and of the organization as a whole.

It is no secret that development of strengths, while recognizing inherent weaknesses, is the best approach in developing employees' natural talents. Peter Drucker wisely suggested that, "A man should never be appointed into a managerial position if his vision focuses on people's weaknesses rather than on their strengths." (Drucker 2006, 157) People never forget the way they have been treated. Praising their best qualities is rewarded many times over.

A strong culture doesn't tolerate inconsistency from different levels of management. People are more encouraged when they can see that their leader is following and contributing to his or her own policies. While demanding an atmosphere of trust, a leader must himself be trustworthy; to maintain professionalism, the leader must himself be a professional. Innovativeness can flourish if the leader is creative and appreciates creativity in others; collective accountability is possible if leaders are themselves accountable, and so on. A double standard that places management "above the law" will backfire every time. For instance, a leader who pushes people to behave unprofessionally toward customers should expect a similar behavior of employees in return. Double standards are properties of a dictatorship, not of a successful and growing organizational culture.

Mastery of modern leadership can be achieved only by the masterful management of human qualities, cultural values, and metaphysical resources. In turn, this demands a leader to be a servant, not a boss. Actually, choosing to be a leader is a choice to serve others. Choosing to serve oneself results in being a boss in charge of a Dark Kingdom organization.

Leaders and bosses have different scales of vision and view leadership's responsibilities differently. Leaders exhibit superiority in vision, competencies, and take responsibility for their actions. From the people servant standpoint, responsibilities are given to him to develop people's values to the highest possible level. A boss has a short-sighted vision, typically of money only, where employees are viewed as expendable and preferably speechless instruments. Their vision is narrow and unappealing.

The leader, as a servant, cares for his employees and can be counted on to be by their side helping them feel supported and valued. A boss sees himself as a king on a throne, promoting only his own superiority. A boss who is not responsive to the people's aims and desires becomes an enemy of own employees and customers.

Actually, what does leadership in the Dark Kingdom look like? It is still outwardly professional, but people are not taken into account. All internal systems look advanced. However, they are unfriendly to employees, and lead to their active undermining of the organization in response to poor treatment.

When a boss seems to only support and praise a particular few, it appears that the boss doesn't see valuable qualities in others, exploring only a portion of the company's potential, causing unbalanced and subjective management. Not surprisingly, in such an organization, employees may even be viewed as obstacles to making money.

In a counterproductive culture, people work in an atmosphere of fear and demoralization. Fear is a bad motivator which creates narrow-minded employees. There is little chance for loyalty, job satisfaction, or respect in such an environment. Sacrificing people for the sake of one's own ambition is as destructive as playing Russian roulette.

Trust a Leader

The trust given to a leader is a special issue. Trusting a leader means employees can concentrate on their duties being sure that their future prospects are secured. Thus, trust in a leader is very crucial factor which defines the quality of relationships in a company. Trust is gained over time and based on experience of the past, thus becoming a predictor of future behavior in the leader.

Trust is definitive leadership quality. Finnish researcher Tarja Ketola (2006, 7-12) explains that trusting a leader depends on the relationship between the leader's values, words, and actions. This must be consistent to earn the trust of employees. If they don't trust the leader, it is because the declared values, words, and actions are inconsistent, and people become aware of such inconsistencies. They cannot place their trust in a leader from whom they don't know what to expect.

People trust consistency more than vision. Positive consistency breeds confidence, and assuages the doubts of employees. Trusting a leader means relying on his or her leadership qualities, despite knowing that no one is perfect and mistakes are possible. Distrust in a leader casts doubt on the meaningfulness of duties and orders coming from the top.

Trust reflects fair dealing with employees and a willingness to give back to them. They will stand for a trusted leader in any challenge. If the leader is not trustworthy, employees will be unwilling to stick with such person and the organization through difficult periods.

Leader's Competencies

The Knowledge Era we live in demands different qualities and competencies in leaders than the previous Industrial Era. The concept of leadership in which the primary task is managing people's behavior is outdated. Focusing on people and their value as a unique asset is far more effective. This demands being a people-servant, with a clear understanding of the leaders' responsibilities to serve employees, in order to maximize their performance and achieve organizational goals.

Modern organizations are up against adaptive challenges which weren't known mere decades ago. Thus, effective leadership demands new competencies and skills, while rethinking traditional ones. This is a straight forward pattern of action – identifying a company's goals and ensuring quality leaders who work for their people, are actively involved and are prepared to go that 'extra mile' themselves in helping their employees achieve success in the organization. Leadership has become more complex, and qualities and competencies such as emotional and cultural intelligence became compulsory parts of the modern leader's profile.

Emotional Intelligence

To manage values, a leader has to be adept at recognizing people's emotions and feelings, knowing their goals, and knowing what best motivates them. In order to guide an employee's thinking, the leader should be highly skilled in emotional intelligence. A dictionary of psychology (Coleman 2008, 282) defines emotional intelligence as the ability to monitor one's own and other people's emotions, to discriminate between different emotions and label them appropriately, and to use emotional information to guide thinking and behavior. Being emotionally intelligent means being aware of how one's own actions and display of emotions might affect others. It is displaying responsiveness, empathy, and supportive emotions which enhance formal and informal human relations. Employing emotional intelligence increases a leader's ability to concentrate employees' energy and effort, and thus to generate success.

We can recall King David, an epic figure with a unique sense for people that allowed him to achieve amazing things. He wasn't perfect, but was a master of his own emotions and a great listener who received much praise from his people for the way he treated them.

American psychologist, Daniel Goleman in his *Emotional Intelligence* (Goleman 2006,

25-170), defined five elements that form emotional intelligence:

- Self-Awareness. People with high emotional intelligence are honest in judging and understanding their own emotions and don't allow them to take control. Self-awareness is associated with confidence and strong intuition resulting in better performance.

- Self-Regulation. Self-regulation is the ability to control emotions and impulses. One's impulsive behavior can lead to an overall negative attitude adversely affecting those around him. Thinking before acting is a property of emotionally intelligent people. They are able to say "no" by cognitive reasoning, not based on emotions. You must be able to control yourself, before you can lead others.

- Motivation. People with a high degree of emotional intelligence are motivated to achieve long-term goals. They don't easily give up, making them effective and highly productive.

- Empathy. This is a highly developed ability to comprehend the goals, needs, and perspectives of others. Empathy is an ability to read between the lines, to suspend judgment, and avoid thinking in stereotypes. It is a characteristic which is essential in order to maintain and manage effective relationships. Empathetic people are honest and transparent. They are able to express appreciation for the efforts of others because they are able to recognize the difficulty of tasks not their own.

- Social Skills. These are the critical skills necessary for team building, effective communication, and conflict resolution. Social skills define support, reciprocity, and focus on a collective success.

Like leaders, "bosses" can also be quite masterful in emotional intelligence. The difference is that they may use their skills for manipulating people to work toward goals that can be quite far from those which are deemed morally acceptable.

Cultural Intelligence

While aiming to catch a stellar wind of success, organizations tend to go global. International business is no longer just an accomplishment of large corporations since even small companies are active on the global markets these days. Far away destinations can easily be reached by short plane rides, and an audio and visual conversation with someone on the other side of the world is routine. Remaining Mr. Local is not enough anymore. Companies are becoming the microcosms which need to be led by leaders with high Cultural Intelligence (CQ).

P. Christopher Earley and Soon Ang coined the term cultural intelligence in their book *Cultural Intelligence* (2003) in response to a growing demand for intelligent cross-cultural management, in order to measure and predict cross-cultural performance, or simply, to define how one is able to work in different cultural contexts.

CQ begins with the personal abilities and competencies to adapt to different contexts and situations, to shape thinking and behavior, and to develop a deeper awareness of one's own culture. There are four capabilities that define CQ:

- CQ-Drive defines the motivation to function in culturally diverse settings.

- CQ-Knowledge is a cognitive factor articulating one's knowledge about differences and similarities between one's own culture and those newly explored.

- CQ-Strategy can be taken as a mega-cognition allowing adaptation to different thought processes and practices.

- CQ-Action reflects the appropriateness of one's attitude in different situations and ability to adapt relevant verbal and nonverbal behavior.

Leaders are not born with these competencies, but instead develop them over time. This demands a readiness and willingness to learn with an open mind, to respect other cultures, and to explore cross-cultural experiences. The more one learns and gains experience about other cultures, the higher one's CQ becomes. Cross-cultural competence is based on a passion to explore new horizons. Success in cross-cultural management comes from challenging ambiguities and learning from mistakes which are inevitable in the new environment.

Speaking from my own experience of running international businesses, a leader has to understand his entry point when expanding into a new territory or market. Failing to do so is like coming into someone's house without an invitation. This demands an understanding of and sensitivity to local culture, habits, and norms. One should have the mentality of a researcher, asking questions, but being receptive to the answers (instead of fitting them into a pre-existing narrative), in order to build the necessary understanding.

Often, differences between regions and cultures are trivial. Coffee will taste different in Italy than in Sweden and office routines are much different between the UK and Greece. Others are more substantial such as the different expressions of trust in China verses Germany. Those more significant differences will cause a substantial amount of emotional and social discomfort until you are able to adapt your policies accordingly.

It takes time and courage to acclimate to unfamiliar trains of thought and cultural symbolism. However, working together with locals and learning from them makes it possible to understand the local environment and adapt whatever local wisdom and practices that may be beneficial.

Organizations come to a new market intending to access local resources. An organization's ability to do this will be completely dependent on its ability to build mutually beneficial local relationships.

Lack of cultural intelligence leads to costly mistakes, such as increased transaction costs, friction with local stakeholders, and resistance from the local workforce. A leader without a global mind set will lead a company's foreign expansion to inevitable failure. Expert on global leadership and author of *Bamboo Strong*, David Clive Price suggests "In order to achieve success in overseas markets and in a multicultural setting at home, you need to adopt what I call a 'bamboo mindset'. That means being strong and flexible, able to support an ambitious business plan and your brand's DNA, and yet supple enough to adapt to cultural differences." (Price 2016, 48)

Power Structure

There are several recognized styles of leadership. Whether a given leader's style is autocratic, democratic, strategic, transactional, or another form of leadership, its success largely depends on the leader's performance, quality of human resources, and how well the organization fulfills its purpose.

While there are many styles, for centuries leadership approaches have fallen into one of two main divisions: to concentrate all power in the hands of a few or to distribute it evenly across many. The choice is whether absolute power is to be maintained, possibly at the expense of performance and illusive cultural qualities, or to let culture flourish while potentially relinquishing power.

A leader is up against a triangle of interacting factors – reasons, relationships, and practices, where every point is fairly subjective in its view. Which is better, to build fortresses of authority or to trust one's own people? Which more effectively supports a leaders' status? Which is easier to manage and which is easier to hijack? What does the experience of others show? Two commonly contrasted views of leadership are the Turkish style used in the Osman's times which represents the absolute power of one, and the French style in which a king received the counsel of the hereditary aristocracy. The Turkish style was difficult to conquer but easy to hold afterward, whereas the French one was relatively easy to conquer but difficult to maintain, facing more challenges than profits.

There are two main scenarios people still use while forming the power structure of their organizations. In one, a power structure can be created to fit people into predefined standards and categories similar to any bureaucratic state. This is a typical leader-centered structure. There is little chance for someone creative or atypical to fit into its criteria and their CVs would be immediately trashed, at long-term cost to the organization. Culture in such cases functions only as an instrument of power to exercise over employees. People are only units of profit in this type of power structure.

In such a system, leaders are considered untouchable and unquestionable. They tend to pass their duties of managing culture and other important functions down to mid-level management. Acting in the name of their untouchable superiors, these middle managers also become corrupted. They build a bureaucratic fortress in the name of the "king," but ultimately for themselves. These fortresses are often in fierce competition within the larger organization. This is like the Osman Empire of olden days.

Nineteen-century British politician Lord Acton famously stated in his letter to Mandell Creighton on the 05th of April 1887, "Power tends to corrupt, and absolute power corrupts absolutely." (Figgis and Laurence 1972, 504) A corrupted organization rots from the inside out and can easily be hijacked. The prosperity of such an organization is fleeting at best.

The second scenario is more organic. Each member of this kind of organization is able to make his own contributions. This is a people-centered structure. It assumes that power is delegated evenly across the organization with every manager and employee considered a value creator and invaluable source of energy, knowledge, and competencies. Free-thinkers are welcomed here as long as they are willing to contribute generously to the organization.

Because the leaders' authority is built on respect rather than fear, they can be questioned by their employees. There is no need for middle managers to fight for influence. The system is based on merit, not flattery and power. The leader is supported by people with appropriate experience, mastery in particular fields, and the authority to make decisions at their discretion. People are not just employees; they are the organization's citizens.

This is a flexible, proactive, and people-valuing structure. From a historical point of view, it is like the former Republic of Venice, small, enormously powerful, influential, and progressive in terms of arts, science, and trade. In 1485, the French ambassador and writer, Philippe de Commynes, wrote of Venice (Blanchard 2001, 140), "It is the most splendid city I have ever seen, and the one which governs itself the most wisely." Venice is still praised by its citizens and millions of visitors every year.

It can be difficult to lead such a company as one tends to act more like a servant to the organization than like a king. Leadership in this case assumes real mastery in managing values and qualities, and care of the people. Also, this people-centered power structure requires enormous vision, effort, and time to create. The majority of citizens in such an organization are fully invested in its goals, working enthusiastically for its success.

These two styles of leadership represent a choice of whether or not to trust people. Niccolò Machiavelli suggested, "Therefore the best fortress is to be found in the love of the people, for although you may have fortresses they will not save you if you are hated by the people." (Machiavelli 2003) The choice is bounded by the leader's personality, vision, traits, and patience.

Discussion

Leadership is about the future, near and distant. A leader must look toward the future, seeing the need for a number of small but important changes that allow the company to make a huge leap forward. One such measure might be a hefty bonus at the end of the year; another could be an increased number of new satisfied customers. Such a leap is only possible if human values and qualities are artfully managed along with metaphysical resources.

The future is not an island where a leader lives in isolation. It is a reality built on family, friends, and teamwork. When engaging people in building a future, a leader should allow them to be part of this bright future and consumers of its fruits. People will not enthusiastically follow if they don't see themselves operating within this bright picture.

People curse things unfamiliar to them or that they don't understand. Communicate your vision and ideas clearly and as many times as needed. A leader who can't or won't communicate his ideas will be left alone without followers.

To look to the future presumes a confidence in the present. This has nothing to do with illusive probabilities. It is the everyday effort needed to make any organization successful. Many leaders lose their charisma and drive because they get bogged down in mechanical aspects of the daily routine. They forget about the people behind the data in their daily reports. It is the valuable hard-working citizens of the organization that generate those reports by daily implementing the leader's vision.

A well-known adage, widely attributed as an old Chinese proverb, says, "If you can command yourself, you can command the world." Leaders whose emotions are not kept under control will lose their best employees. This lack of emotional intelligence, leading to a loss of employee loyalty, is costly for the whole organization.

Founders and leaders define organizational culture from the outset, but employees play an instrumental role in allowing it to flourish for the sake of their own well-being and that of the organization. It is after all, the source of their livelihood where they spend a third of their lives. Leadership, in turn, has the daily responsibility to set the example in building up the organization and its culture.

Practical Tips

- Culture reflects the leadership. Leaders need to honestly assess how they are perceived.

- A leader is responsible for the organization's cultural health. The state of the employees depends on whether a leader is building a positive or negative culture.

- Culture grows due to the positive expression of emotional sentiment. Think how you, as a leader fed it today, and imagine how it will reflect on next week's report.

- Leadership is charisma plus pragmatically rational management based on the ability to recognize values.

- Expressing appreciation costs nothing but pays back immensely in positive morale.

- Good leaders are always in great demand because people need leaders' qualities to complement their own. The leader's mission is to serve others and help them grow.

- "Talking head" leaders are a dime a dozen. A real leader's quality is in an ability to open the minds and the hearts of the employees.

- Leaders invest in people. By adding value to people and helping them to realize their qualities, they are becoming better leaders themselves. Know your potential and help people to explore theirs. This is a perpetual cycle – a good leader makes good employees who make him an even better leader.

- Complaining about bad employees is pointless as the leader is either the one who hired them or who neglected their development.

- One word of encouragement can open new horizons for someone. Help employees to explore their potential.

CHAPTER TEN

A WINEMAKER CHECKLIST

Caring of a Perfect Harvest

A glass of perfect wine is always rewarding after a busy week in the office. Full-bodied taste, ruby color, and a noble aftertaste lift our spirit and emotions. Small wonder why some exemplary bottles of wine cost thousands and are praised as pieces of fine art.

Consider that the quality of the wine reflects the performance and character of the winemaker. A good wine reflects high performance, whereas bad wine is a reflection of average or below average performance.

It would be incorrect to assume that a winemaker has an easy life drinking chilled wine while sitting in the shadow of olive trees. The winemaker has clear weekly, monthly, and seasonal schedules imprinted deep into the back of his mind. This bottled perfection of chemistry is built on everyday effort and a clear plan of actions. He works hard, taking care of numerous things which may look strange to someone unfamiliar with this almost mystical process, before his product can be presented to customers as a product of love, not just as a drink. He cares for every single grapevine every day, in any weather, protects them from parasites and diseases, fertilizes the soil, and removes the weeds, in order to allow the vines proper feeding and growth. The good winemaker's employees consider the winery as their own, putting their minds and hearts into the harvest.

Performance matters and proves the effort of every employee was worthwhile and focused on a shared goal. This is the reward for the accomplishments which where stimulated and supported by the organization's culture. Taking care of grapevines is similar to taking care of culture; it is the leaders' choice to care and get a noble wine or not to care and allow the weeds to grow while expecting a good harvest. To reap the fruits of culture, one should have a clear and routinely executed plan of action, designed to avoid problems, organizational diseases, and loss of cultural energy.

Revisions for Strengthening

The flow of an organization's life is fast and ever changing, requiring frequent evaluation of conditions and factors of culture to identify necessary revisions. The aim of the culture's revision is to recognize problems and allow culture to execute its roles and functions as fully as possible. Cultural revision is serious work itself as the amount of information required is large, and any action taken has be done with full commitment and follow through, otherwise, it'll do more harm than good.

What are the signals for revision? Whether you see that processes are driving people rather than the other way around, or your company starts losing the best people, it is time to roll up the sleeves and take care of culture. Culture is a superpower that can be a cause of or solution for most organizational problems.

In simple words, imagine yourself as a buyer of an organization's culture as a product. This is similar to purchasing a company or major share in it. How dear are you prepared to pay for it? Or invest enthusiastically to realize culture's enormous value? The price for culture is nothing less than the whole business.

Employees worldwide are actively disengaged at work and this problem is attributed to organizational culture. According to the Gallup's new State of the Global Workplace report for 2017, only fifteen percent of employees worldwide are engaged in their jobs. Thus, shockingly, eighty-five percent are functioning below their potential in terms of both their value to employers and the sense of fulfillment they derive from their work. In monetary terms, disengaged employees cost the United States' economy somewhere between $450 billion and $550 billion per year. It is too serious an issue to be ignored, but, at the same time, a huge potential pitfall for all businesses.

Before diving into the revision process, one should think about numerous issues and ask many questions. Think as a mature investor, with an objective approach, who takes thoughtful notes on how long an organization's culture can sustain itself and identify chances for improvement in terms of adding value to it. In any case, one should be prepared for a hefty investment of effort, time, and engagement from everyone in the organization.

Where to Start?

Revision begins with determining whether an organization's culture is positive or negative. Leaders form and define culture, but employees, while being contributors, are also consumers of an organization's culture and perhaps the best judges of it. Therefore, it is critical to hear what people think of the culture and their suggestions.

A lot depends on the extent to which culture is cared for and how regularly it is checked. Regular checks allow one to see how culture is developing. This is invaluable for those focused on the future. If culture checks are both frequent and effective there will be little resistance from employees. On the other hand, if this is a novel experience then one must be prepared for cynics and gossips which should be handled delicately.

If the culture is found to be negative, then see it as a great opportunity. It may sound strange, but rising from failure and getting out of the Dark Kingdom is a great way to unite all of an organization's members. Once you break through the initial resistance and demonstrate your own commitment to the organization and the people in it, you will receive the strongest possible support and appreciation from employees. People are inherently keen to leave a positive mark upon the world, so they will appreciate being part of building an encouraging and supportive environment which erases much of the memory of the dark times. The Dark Kingdom gives people nothing but fear whereas positive culture gives people fresh hope. Changing that fear to hope is difficult but can give the organization a vitality it may not have had since its beginnings.

The extent to which people are aware of the organization's vision, goals, and values defines what they will bring to the company - their best qualities and strengths or worries and weaknesses. Cultural management is nothing but a waste of time if people are not aware of such cornerstones as symbols and values of the organization.

Employees' Engagement

Responsibility for the culture falls not only on leaders but on employees as well. Employees are culture residents with relevant duties and responsibilities, not just disinterested spectators. However, they need support from leaders. Thus, it is critical to ask if the employees' values, goals, and qualities are being recognized by the company. In what manner are the employees supported?

Employees contribute their time, values, and qualities to an organization through engagement which, as a result, is directly correlated with performance. People will become engaged if they are confident that the organization and its culture are contributing to their own success. Their goals should be linked to the company's goals. Referring to the Gallup's report (2017), employees who strongly agree that they can link their goals to the organization's goals are 3.5 times more likely to be engaged.

Revision should reveal what restricts people from personal growth and satisfaction while working for a company. Positive culture is a meeting point in which collaboration with others leads to employees' continual positive development. That creates a feedback loop in which their own engagement increases, as does their personal stake in the organization, which in turn improves the environment even more. A negative culture works much the same way, with the result that the organization becomes an ever more unpleasant place to work.

Communication is one of the most critical functions of culture and must be checked carefully. It has a direct impact on performance. First and foremost, communication is an interaction with others. People prefer to interact through actions and messages that create a sense of engagement with other people. Thus, by active communication, employees are nourishing culture which thrives off those relationships. Positive culture is definitely not deaf or mute.

Employees want to talk about their performance, growth, and involvement. This is an absolutely normal desire for anyone. The seemingly simple issue of helping people to understand the purpose of their work through regular communication and discussions with peers and managers has a dramatic impact on their motivation and, as a result, on their performance.

Communication defines the development of effective relationships, whether internal or external. The state of internal relationships for an organization is crucial for shared camaraderie and support. It is also a prerequisite for the development of metaphysical resources which are in turn the product of collective actions. The strength of internal relationships is reflected in the quality of external relationships such as customer service and transactions with the organization's partners.

Intensiveness of communication between hierarchical levels reflects the responsiveness and accessibility of leaders and managers, tacit understanding between employees, and unity of the organization as one body. Vision, goals, values, and the concern of leaders about their employees can't be transmitted to all employees if inconsistencies of communication exist between hierarchical levels. There are a few questions which can help to reveal communication problems:

- How productive and supportive is the nature of internal relationships?

- What are the main subjects of discussions among employees? Their roles, duties, growth, or something not relevant to company life?

- How do employees communicate with external stakeholders?

- How accessible are leaders and senior managers?

State of Metaphysical Resources

The role of metaphysical resources goes beyond conventional understanding; bounded by the common feeling of time and space and defining the existence of an organization as a living being. Therefore, a reservoir of metaphysical resources must be checked regularly.

A revision of the state of metaphysical resources begins with simple questions: Whether the organization is realizing the critical role of metaphysical resources or not; how systematically they are cared for, or if care is characterized by ad hoc actions. This has a direct impact on the state of metaphysical resources – strong and constantly growing or demanding development. There is no such thing as an average or tolerable state of metaphysical resources. Average or tolerable means that they are not properly cared for or recognized as having a critical role in the organization's existence. It is not enough to develop one of the metaphysical resources while ignoring others. In an organizational context, real trust can't be developed without shared vision and accountability, or professionalism without innovativeness. They are only effective when developed together.

Development of metaphysical resources is the shared responsibility of all employees and not limited by the duties of a designated manager or marketing department. Thus, it will be logical to ask who takes care of them and how regularly. If they are not cared for, then it will be logical to ask

- what are the managers and leaders in the company actually doing?

The Role of Management

The way managers treat the core values of employees, customers, and all other stakeholders defines sustained financial performance. Productive culture is a prerequisite for adding economic value to the company. However, despite trendy discussions about the importance of culture management, it seems that managers still struggle to find time to even talk with their own people. Care of culture on paper, but not in practice, leads to wasting time managing an illusion, consequently demotivating employees. These managers are hiding their heads in the sand instead of reacting and solving their culture's problems.

Try to ask managers about their leadership style and everyone will tell you that they are leaders not bosses. Unfortunately, this is far from being true. Good revision is based on honest answers. Change assumes the active involvement of all in the company. Improvement begins not with employees but with leaders and managers whose positive input into a company's culture should be visible to their employees.

Caring for the culture of an organization means more than putting up well-produced posters with clever slogans. It means more than having meetings in which managers read some slides from a presentation to their employees. These things do not inspire. Rather, employees should be directly involved in setting the goals of the organization and/or their workgroup whenever possible.

Employees involved in setting the organization's goals are more likely to be engaged in an organization's life and development as feeling responsible and directly involved. However, in practice, only a minor percentage of employees is involved in setting their organization's goals or is even aware of them. This is purely the fault of managers who do not realize they are losing an important source of inner energy. By asking simple questions, leaders can realize a lot about their role and actual involvement in culture management.

- What is your management style? Are you a leader who takes care of people or a boss taking care of yourself?
- Who takes care of culture in a company?
- What is the input of leaders and managers into culture?
- Are employees aware of leaders' goals and values?
- How do you recognize and stimulate subordinates' values, qualities, and talents?
- In what ways do leaders show they care about their employees' successes?

It all hinges on whether leaders are leading people to success or restricting their growth, and in so doing putting the company's development into jeopardy.

Change

Preparedness and ability to change define an organization's fitness in an ever-changing environment. Life moves at an incredibly fast pace, leaving rigid companies far behind to suffer a slow death. Daily, it demands new qualities, competencies, and skills. There should be no doubt about the necessity to change.

Change is not a spontaneous action, but a focused response to the environment's demands. Change is a journey with a defined starting point and a final goal. Otherwise, it is just wandering in uncertainty without any profit for a company and its employees. The trip begins with the realization that there is a necessity for change, followed by setting clear goals, and ends when those goals are achieved. To help this process go as smoothly as possible, it is important to understand lessons learned from previous periods of change.

What were the aims and results of the most recent changes implemented in your company? What caused that change? What were the employees' reactions to those changes? This may sound obvious, but these questions help to understand the ability to recognize the triggers of change and focus on the most critical aspects, and to comprehend the organization's overall responsiveness to change.

Scarcity of resources is not an excuse to avoid change. By limiting the ability to perform due to a perceived lack of necessary resources, a company is condemning itself. Change demands a thoroughly crafted plan which allows implementation even when only limited resources are available. The longest journey begins with the first few steps. Even small, frequent change is always cheaper than dramatic losses in the future. Should the culture turn negative, the losses will be far greater.

Change can't be implemented without supporters. Seek out those who have successfully supported changes in the past. Using their experience will help with future changes. It also lets these employees know that you value their input and efforts. These enthusiasts may also identify opportunities for improvement and will support the necessary changes in the future.

A Tool for Everyday Use

Culture will flourish if cared for. Like a grapevine, it demands constant nourishment and pruning. Forget to clear the weeds off for a few days and grapevines will suffer, turning wild and bringing a poor harvest. Neglect culture and the roots of cynicism, laziness, and deception will develop.

This chapter is designed to provide a culture management checklist which leaders and entrepreneurs can use as a tool and apply routinely, confident that the main issues of culture are being considered. Feelings and emotions can't be measured by using metrics, but only through a sophisticated understanding of what people experience as part of the organization's culture. Therefore, when analyzing and managing organizational culture, one becomes a psychologist, healer, and researcher who discovers the nature of the company's culture and its peculiarities by asking appropriate questions and by daily observing those in the workforce.

Discussion

No organization is perfect. All have experienced downturns the same as individual people. Those times may bring sad memories but the lessons learned are invaluable. Leaders and employees learn how to rise above problems by mobilizing their inner resources and uniting together. Strong culture allows an organization to withstand harsh times and recover its market position like a phoenix rising from ashes becoming stronger every time.

A successful corporate strategy is built on issues of social identity, functions, and the roles of every employee. Tomorrow's achievements are built on the everyday improvement of people's competencies and qualities. A company can't move further than its employees' competencies, strategic development is bounded by development of people and their values. Thus an organization's growth demands investment into people and care of the team that makes the business function on a daily basis.

Every human has cancer cells which, if triggered, can destroy a body. The same applies to an organization in which everyone has the cells of conflict which are embedded in the organization's DNA. Inner cultural incompatibilities trigger those cells, provoking larger conflicts. At the same time, a strong culture is the most effective mediator of inner conflicts. Otherwise, a weak and dysfunctional culture will only fuel conflicts.

Modern commerce assumes that being socially responsible is a taken-for-granted requirement for any customer-focused organization. Social responsibility is a mandatory requirement for those thinking about customers' needs and their living environments. Their product is wrapped in the care of people. The social responsibility of a business is a bridge which a company builds with a society and by doing so, gains more customers.

Culture does not disappear when an organization goes out of business. The signs of it can be seen in the leaders' new businesses. One who closes one company will likely develop the same cultural pattern in a new venture unless having learned how to build it differently and stronger. People are carriers of culture's seeds, seeds that reside in all of us. By changing jobs and companies, people spread their understanding of culture imprinted by previous experience far from the initial soil from which it sprang.

Culture is a measure of success and a cause of it; it is a desire for success and a way to it; a reality and a secured future at the same time, which demands everyday attention. If one is trying to hold it in the iron gloves of rules, culture turns negative as creativity is stifled and prevented from stimulating cultural growth. Ignore values for the sake of rules - and the bottom line will decrease. What is the price for not taking appropriate care of culture? The answer is nothing less than your business.

CHAPTER ELEVEN

THE MAGIC COLORS
OF THE FUTURE

The main competencies of the last century were focused on handling technology. Notions of managing human values and qualities were met with skepticism rather than with serious attention and practical application. Twenty years ago, it was a risky approach taken by only a few. Today, the direct relation between performance and culture cannot be denied.

We are well into the Knowledge Era and this is a time for new thinking about people and their values, and appreciating that everyone has a stake in building the future. People have learned that real development is more important than immediate profit, and excellence is only in people, not in machines. People-centered approaches have already proved their advantages and viability. We are moving into an age of using different metrics in business than have been used in the last few decades.

According to the United Nations projection, the world's population is expected to be 9.8 billion people by 2050. A number of companies will grow enormously and the pressure to compete in the growing and rapidly changing marketplace will only increase. This will be an era of competition of cultures and cultural systems, not processes. Managing them and fulfilling their demands will be more difficult than ever and will only be possible for those who have built a strong culture. Those organizations will be focused on maintaining strong culture and development of know-how in culture management which will allow the constant development of the values and qualities of their people.

Culture accompanies and influences every aspect of organizational activities, from risk evaluation to being a socially responsible company, to deciding in which areas the company should grow. Metaphysical resources will be invaluable assets of any advanced organization looking to succeed in the future.

A Corporate Culture Officer will be a forthcoming necessity, whose job will be focusing on people inside and outside the organization and merging their qualities. This is not about being a utopian corporation but about becoming stronger and better performing. Culture management is a special trait of progressive top and senior managers which demands relevant qualifications and competencies.

We are not hunting mammoths with stone axes anymore. We are taking care of people by offering them corporate products and services. The only similarity that remains constant over ages is the need for teamwork. Whether we are talking about the digital transformation of marketing, or taking down the mammoth, teamwork is essential. The computers, like spears, that are used are only tools.

Metaphysical resources are formed by people. If metaphysical resources are properly cultivated, people will be led by values rather than rules that restrict innovation and sap employees' willingness to perform. The soft but unstoppable power of a strong culture influences everyone directly, encourages personal growth, and provides social comfort to each organization's member. It provides the opportunity and an appropriate environment to push one's self to new limits. This is one of the highest morale missions of the contemporary business.

The best investment for the future is taking care of your organization's driving superpower, culture, becoming a people servant. Every human is a universe unto himself; thus, his energy is desperately needed to progress your corporation, whether it is big or small. If leaders want their organizations to perform above the ordinary, then they should think culture, speak culture, nurture culture, and live culture.

Business is stepping into an age of V2V (values-to-values) approaches, i.e. transferring values from people in an organization to its customers. B2B (business-to-business) and B2C (business-to-customers) approaches are no longer sufficient. It is necessary to maintain a level of organic interface between users and producers through matching the values and desires of both parties involved. At present, we are talking about value-management assuming its application is to employees only. Very soon, we will be talking about matching the values of organization's members and customers and thus, achieving superior synergy by getting customers involved in value creation. We already are doing such things while having only a vague understanding of the nature of such processes, for instance, through different online services or social media. How a person feels after dealing with an organization, whether as an employee or customer, matters more every day and will be critical for the decades ahead.

Cultural maintenance doesn't tolerate only a partial effort. It can't be dropped halfway through. Do it effectively resulting in success or leave it underperforming and, as a result, ruin the expectations of all those who supported you. Such a failure, primarily as a result of the organization's leaders, will inevitably lead to the future creation of Dark Kingdom organizations. Such choices culminate in losing in competition and in the resulting lack of quality human resources. The grey and black colors of the Dark Kingdom won't match with the bright blues, oranges, and greens of the future.

Entering into this new era, we are changing how to apply an organization's forces. This means shifting mental paradigms, both with regard to management's outward worldview, as well as self-introspection, in order to see the values and qualities that others bring to the organization. This creates space for the exploration of new horizons and opportunities.

However, business is responsible for what is created as much as for what is left behind. Whether it is a scorched land and stagnating markets or fond memories and satisfied customers depend on the culture of organizations. Therefore, building a strong culture is building a confident future for everyone impacted by the organization, and thus, each party should be involved by contributing to teamwork, trust, innovativeness, professionalism, and accountability. This is a collective responsibility for all businesses.

REFERENCES

- Aristotle. 2012. *Nicomachean Ethics*. New York: Dover Publications. Kindle.

- Blanchard, Jöel, Ed. 2001. *Philippe de Commynes, Lettres*. Geneva: Droz.

- Cheang, Jennifer. 2017. "Manufacturing, Retail, and Food and Beverage Industries Rank Worst for Workplace Mental Health." *Mental Health America*. October 11, 2017. Accessed January 30, 2018. http://www.mentalhealthamerica.net/blog/manufacturing-retail-and-food-and-beverage-industries-rank-worst-workplace-mental-health

- Coleman, Andrew. 2008. *A Dictionary of Psychology* (3rd Ed.). Oxford: Oxford University Press.

- Covey, Stephen R. 2013. *The 7 Habits of Highly Effective People: Powerful Lessons in Personal Change*. London: Simon & Schuster.

- Crabtree, Steve. 2018. "Global Productivity Hinges on Human Capital Development." *Gallup News*. Accessed February 2, 2018.

http://news.gallup.com/topic/employee_
engagement.aspx

- Dalberg-Acton, John Emerich Edward. *Historical Essays and Studies.* 1907 Ed. Figgis, Neville John, and Reginald Vere Laurence. *Essays on Freedom and Power.* 1972. accessed July 15, 2017. https://mises. org/sites/default/files/Essays%20on%20 Freedom%20and%20Power_3.pdf

- Drucker, Peter F. 1963. "Managing for Business Effectiveness." *Harvard Business Review*, May 1963. Boston: Harvard Business Publishing. Accessed February 6, 2017. https://hbr.org/1963/05/ managing-for-business-effectiveness

- Drucker, Peter F. 1991. "Don't Change Corporate Culture: Use It." *The Wall Street Journal*, March 1991.

- Drucker, Peter F. 2006. *The Practice of Management.* New York: Harper Business.

- Earley, P. Christopher, and Soon Ang. 2003. *Cultural Intelligence: Individual Interactions Across Cultures.* California: Stanford University Press.

- Einstein, Albert. 2009. *Einstein on Cosmic Religion and Other Opinions and Aphorisms.* New York: Dover Publication.

- Goethe, Johann Wolfgang. "The way you see people is the way you treat them, and the way you treat them is what they become." Accessed November 18, 2017. https://www.brainyquote.com/quotes/ johann_wolfgang_von_goeth_378590

* Goldsmith, Marshall, and Mark Reiter. 2015. *Triggers: Sparking Positive Change and Making it Last*. London: Profile Books.

* Goleman, Daniel. 2006. *Emotional Intelligence*. New York: Bantam.

* Goll, Irene, and B. Rakesh Sambharaya. 1995. "Corporate Ideology, Diversification and Firm Performance." *Organization Studies*, 16/5 (1995): 823-846.

* Hofstede, Geert. 1980. *Culture's consequences: International Differences in Work-related Values*. Beverly Hills: Sage.

* James, William. 1880. "Great Men, Great Thoughts, and the Environment." Lecture delivered before the Harvard Natural History Society. Atlantic Monthly. October 1880. Accessed December 15, 2017. https://www. uky.edu/~eushe2/Pajares/jgreatmen.html

* Jung, Carl G. 1976. *Jung Letters, 1951- 1961, Vol. 2*. Princeton, New Jersey: Princeton University Press.

* Jung, Carl G. 1989. *Memories, Dreams, Reflections*. Reissue edition. London: Vintage, Penguin.

- Kaufman, Scott Barry. 2016. "Both Introverts and Extraverts Get Exhausted from Too Much Socializing." *Scientific American*. June 14, 2016. Accessed September 12, 2017. **https://blogs. scientificamerican.com/beautiful-minds/ both-introverts-and-extraverts-get- exhausted-from-too-much-socializing/**

- Ketola, Tarja. 2006. "Do You Trust Your Boss? A Jungian Analysis of Leadership Reliability in CSR." *Electronic Journal of Business Ethics and Organization Studies*. Vol. 11, No. 2. Accessed June 15, 2015.

- **http://citeseerx.ist.psu.edu/viewdoc/down- load?doi=10.1.1.112.7704&rep=rep1&- type=pdf**

- Konovalov, Oleg. 2016. *Organisational Anatomy*. New Castle: Cambridge Scholars Publishing.

- Lao, Tzu. *Tao Te Ching*. 1993. Indianapolis: Hackett Classics.

- Lewin, Kurt, Ronald Lippitt, and Ralph K. White. 1939. "Patterns of Aggressive Behavior in Experimentally Created Social Climates." *Journal of Social Psychology*, 10 (1939): 271-299.

- Machiavelli, Niccolò. 2003. *The Prince*. 1 edition. Harlow: Longman. Kindle.

- Mandelshtam, Osip. 1973. *Complete Poetry of Osip Emilevich Mandelstam.* New York: State University of New York Press.
- Maslach, Christina. 1982. "Understanding Burnout: Definitional Issues in Analyzing a Complex Phenomenon." In W. S. Paine (Ed.), *Job Stress and Burnout* (pp. 29-40). Beverly Hills: Sage Publications.
- Mattone, John, and Nick Vaidya. 2016. *Cultural Transformations: Lessons of Leadership and Corporate Reinvention.* New Jersey: Wiley Publishing.
- Neller, Robert B. 2017. (@ GenRobertNeller), "Just signed my page 11. Online = extension of uniformed presence. Our discipline to orders is what sets us apart. Accessed April 04, 2017. https://go.usa.gov/xX5SZ
- Plait, Phil. 2010. "The Goal of Skepticism, Don't Be a Dick." Accessed August 18, 2017. https://www.youtube.com/watch?v=ucDXvXqr_H8
- Price, David Clive. 2016. *Bamboo Strong: Cultural Intelligence Secrets to Succeed in the New Global Economy.* London: DCP Global Limited.
- Satoro, Ryunosuke. "Individually, we are one drop. Together, we are an ocean."

Accessed May 14, 2017. http://izquotes.
com/quote/163045

- Sheridan, John E. 1992. "Organizational Culture and Employee Retention." *The Academy of Management Journal*, Vol. 35, No. 5 (1992), pp. 1036-1056.

- Sinek, Simon. 2017. *Find Your Why: A Practical Guide for Discovering Purpose for You and Your Team.* London: Portfolio, Penguin Random House.

- Sun Tzu. 2008. *The Art of War.* London: Penguin Random House. Kindle.

- The Holy Bible. 1992. The Good News Translation (2nd ed., Luke 16:10–11). New York: American Bible Society.

- United Nations Department of Economic and Social Affairs. 2017. "World Population Projected to Reach 9.8 Billion in 2050, and 11.2 Billion in 2100." Accessed August 25, 2017. https://www.un.org/development/desa/en/news/population/world-population-prospects-2017.html

Word-of-mouth is critical to an author's long-term success. If you appreciated this book please leave a review on the Amazon sales page:

http://wbp.bz/CSpowera

For More News About Oleg Konovalov Signup For Our Newsletter:

http://wbp.bz/newsletter

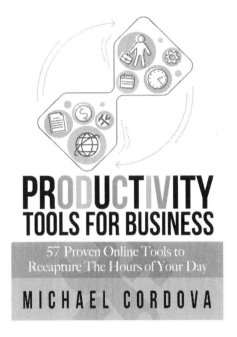

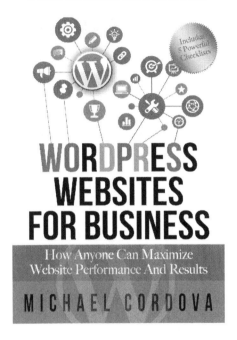

The Importance of Long-Tail Keywords, Intent and the Mobile Factor

When you use keyword phrases consisting of several words in them you have a much better chance of getting ranked for those keyword phrases. Not only that, you can incorporate the users intent in them. For example, let's say you were selling golf clubs. See the following keywords and note how the search terms get more specific and show more intent as you go down:

golf – Someone killing time on their computer

golf clubs – Someone doing general research for golf clubs

pitching wedge – Someone doing general research on pitching wedges

ping G30 driver deals – Someone looking to buy a Ping G30 driver

When doing your keyword research you need to think about what intent you are looking to capture, what specific types of products and services you *want to* provide. Of course it varies by the type of company. Here are some examples of long-tail keywords with intent to engage or purchase:

small business cpa firm to reduce our taxes

auto mechanic to fix my 2017 jeep grand cherokee transmission

chiropractor specializing in a stiff neck

whole roasted pig with green chile catering service (I must be getting hungry)

You need to keep the long-tail and intent concepts in mind when you do your keyword research and write your content. This refinement will make a huge difference in your results. In the above examples, if you instead had focused on cpa firm, auto mechanic, chiropractor or catering service then you'll not only *not be* targeting your company's specific services, but you'll be attempting to rank for keywords that are the most difficult to get top organic rankings for.

Now that we have really smart phones that you can just ask questions of like the Apple Siri or the Android "Ok Google..." capability, and devices like the Amazon Echo (Alexa) and Google Home, search engine queries are now being slanted to those coming from these devices. Now queries like these are becoming more important:

"Ok Google, what's the best Mexican restaurant near me?"

"Alexa, what are the best local activities for kids"

"What are the best local coffee shops"

People are searching on their mobile devices in a hands-free scenario looking for a service that they can use now. *They're on the way!* You need to think about these concepts when you compile your list of keywords that you'll be targeting for your website content.

The Best Tools to Find Long-Tail Keywords

Google again provides great methods and tools to acquire highly relevant long-tail keywords. Since it is Google rankings that you are after, taking Google's suggestions is getting your keywords straight from the horse's mouth.

Do a Google search for your topic and pay attention to the search terms that Google suggests in the search box:

Next, scroll down to the bottom of the results of your search and note the other terms (long-tail keywords) that Google suggests for you:

Searches related to concrete contractor

concrete **contractors denver**	**commercial** concrete **contractors denver**
concrete **delivery denver**	**good day** concrete
residential concrete **denver**	**denver** concrete **prices**
denver concrete **services**	**sunny day** concrete

Grab the keyword phrases that are relevant to your current needs and use them in your article. If you need more then recycle - take the relevant ones and use them in another search to get more suggestions.

A favorite tool among marketers is UberSuggest.io. You just type in a seed keyword, and it gives you a ton of other keywords by appending words to your seed keyword starting with each letter of the alphabet. The video at the bottom of the page shows you how to copy and paste these keywords to a spreadsheet and use all of their basic functions.

Another quick source of long-tail keywords is http://soovle. com. Just type in your keyword and they'll list relevant options from Google, Bing, Yahoo!, Wikipedia, Youtube, Answers.com and Amazon.

Many more keyword tools are available in the free download that you can grab from the Resources section at the end of this book.

Use Qualified, Prioritized Keywords to Drive Compelling Content

Once you have completed the above, then you have the information you need to start mapping out your website content. Create a Wordpress category for each of the categories in the spreadsheet. If a category is too broad, then break it down into multiple categories of finer detail. Sort the spreadsheet by two columns - priority then category. This provides you with the keywords most relevant to your business and the topics (categories) that you can provide solutions for. Next create a list of solutions representing a series of posts for each of the categories. You don't have to write the content now, just a list of concepts/solutions that you'll write about. This list will be your content map for future blog posts. Think in terms of problems that your customers are looking to solve, and solutions that you have already provided *or can provide.*

Ask each member of your team to make a list of the solutions they have provided for customers, then drop each one into the most relevant category. Doing this will provide a great inventory of blog posts that are targeted to solving your customers problems *with your company's priorities built-in.* They'll be customer-centric in terms of solutions to their problems, and they'll be focusing on keywords that are a priority to your business with a great chance of getting rankings and traffic from them.

This is huge, so if you didn't grasp this concept stop now. Go back and read it again. This is all of the content you'll ever need for your website. As you continue to provide solutions, add more content.

Wordpress Websites For Business details
http://wbp.bz/ww4b